1979

The Fantastic Art of Vienna

The Fantastic Art of Vienna

ALESSANDRA COMINI

Alfred A. Knopf
New York 1978

THIS IS A BORZOI BOOK
PUBLISHED BY ALFRED A. KNOPF, INC.

Manufactured in the United States of America

First Edition: October 1978

Front cover illustrations:
Above left: Detail, *Love-Couple,* Wolfgang Hutter.
  Private collection.
Right: Detail, *Hope (I),* Gustav Klimt. The National Gallery,
  Ottawa.
Below left: *Moses and the Angel of the Lord Before the
  Burning Bush,* Ernst Fuchs. Bundesministerium für
  Unterricht, Vienna.
Right: *The Ark of Odysseus,* Rudolf Hausner. Historisches
  Museum der Stadt Wien.

Back cover illustration:
  War and Peace Can Be Pulled On and Off Like Gloves, Erich
  Brauer. Collection Jean Aberbach, New York.

Library of Congress Cataloging in Publication Data

Comini, Alessandra.
  The fantastic art of Vienna.

  Includes index.
  1. Magic realism (Art)—Austria—Vienna.
2. Art, Austrian—Austria—Vienna. 3. Art, Modern—
20th century—Austria—Vienna. I. Title.
N6808.5.M3C65   1978   759.36'13   78-54886
ISBN 0-394-50263-9

To
Dollie
and
Viktor
Fogarassy

Acknowledgments

The idea for this book came from Paul Anbinder, energetic vice-president of Ballantine Books, who persuaded this at first reluctant author that after four books on Klimt and Schiele she still had more to say about Vienna. I should like to thank my New York editor Lynne Williams Bair for her editorial doggedness and finesse and Nan Richardson for her persistence in tracking down capricious photographic sources. I am indebted to Hildegarde Bachert and Dr. Otto Kallir of the Galerie St. Etienne in New York for their customary generous assistance. In Austria I should like to acknowledge the gracious cooperation of the artist Hans Fronius, who created a "fantastic" portrait especially for this book, and in Dallas I am indebted as always to the fine-toothed editorial comb of my mother, Professor Emerita Megan Laird Comini. A summer grant from Dean George Zeiss' University College Council on the Humanities of Southern Methodist University provided the research opportunities for the ideas presented here.

Contents

List of
Illustrations

List of Plates

BLACK AND WHITE

1 Albrecht Altdorfer (c. 1480–1538)
The Wild People of the Woods, c. 1510. Pen and chalk drawing. Albertina, Vienna.

2 Anton Pilgram (c. 1460–c. 1515)
Self-Portrait of the Sculptor, c. 1514–1515. Carved stone pulpit. St. Stephen's Cathedral, Vienna.

3 Franz Anton Maulbertsch (1724–1796)
Self-Portrait, c. 1760. Oil. Osterreichische Galerie, Vienna.

4 Franz Xaver Messerschmidt (1736–1783)
Self-Portraits Grimacing, 1776–1783. Marble and lead. Osterreichische Galerie, Vienna.

5 Franz Xaver Messerschmidt (1736–1783)
Self-Portrait Grimacing, 1776–1783. Marble. Osterreichische Galerie, Vienna.

6 Ferdinand Georg Waldmüller (1793–1865)
The Roman Ruins in Schönbrunn Castle Park, 1832. Oil. Osterreichische Galerie, Vienna.

7 Moritz von Schwind (1804–1871)
The Erl King, c. 1830. Oil. Osterreichische Galerie, Vienna.

8 Josef Danhauser (1805–1845)
The Art Critics (Dog Comedy), 1841. Oil. Historisches Museum der Stadt Wien.

9 August von Pettenkofen (1822–1889)
Gypsy Thief Chased by Dogs, 1871. Oil. Osterreichische Galerie, Vienna.

10 Gustav Klimt (1862–1918)
Jurisprudence, 1903–1907. Oil. Formerly Osterreichische Galerie, Vienna, destroyed by fire, 1945.

11 Rudolf Jettmar (1869–1939)
Lucifer Leaving Cain to His Fate, 1919–1920. Etching. Ostdeutsche Galerie, Regensburg.

12 Rudolf Jettmar (1869–1939)
Prehistoric Monsters on the Road to Hell, 1919–1920. Etching. Ostdeutsche Galerie, Regensburg.

13 Max Oppenheimer ("Mopp") (1885–1954)
Bleeding Man (Self-Portrait), 1911. Oil. University of Kansas Art Museum, Lawrence.

14 Albert Paris von Gütersloh (1887–1973)
Self-Portrait at the Easel, 1913. Oil. Historisches Museum der Stadt Wien.

15 Alfred Kubin (1877–1959)
Self-Portrait Vignettes Around a Photograph of the Artist, 1921. Pencil. Present whereabouts unknown.

16 Alfred Kubin (1877–1959)
The Swamp, c. 1900. Pen and wash drawing. Neue Galerie Linz, Austria. Photo: Spangenberg Verlag, Munich.

17 Alfred Kubin (1877–1959)
Mother Earth, 1900. Pen, ink, wash, stipple on "kataster" paper. Private collection. Courtesy Serge Sabarsky Gallery.

18 Alfred Kubin (1877–1959)
Pipehead, 1945. Aquatint. Private collection. Courtesy Serge Sabarsky Gallery.

19 Hans Fronius (b. 1903)
Struck by Blindness, 1977. Etching. Private collection.

COLOR

1 Ferdinand Georg Waldmüller (1793–1865)
Boy With Lantern, 1824. Oil. Kunsthalle, Hamburg.

2 Moritz von Schwind (1804–1871)
Rubezahl, 1851. Oil. Osterreichische Galerie, Vienna.

3 Moritz von Schwind (1804–1871)
The Virgin, 1860. Oil. Schack-Galerie, Munich.

4 Moritz von Schwind (1804–1871)
Erwin von Steinbach's Dream, c. 1859. Oil. Schack-Galerie, Munich.

5 Anton Romako (1832–1889)
The Hot Springs of Gastein in Festival Illumination, 1877. Oil. Osterreichische Galerie, Vienna.

6 Anton Romako (1832–1889)
Admiral Tegetthoff in the Sea Battle at Lissa, c. 1880. Oil. Osterreichische Galerie, Vienna.

7 Hans Makart (1840–1884)
The Death of Cleopatra, 1876. Oil. Staatliche Kunstsammlungen, Kassel.

8 Rudolf von Alt (1812–1905)
Hans Makart's Studio, 1885. Watercolor. Historisches Museum der Stadt Wien.

9 Giovanni Segantini (1858–1899)
The Evil Mothers, 1894. Oil. Kunsthistorisches Museum, Vienna.

10 Giovanni Segantini (1858–1899)
The Evil Mothers, detail, 1894. Oil. Kunsthistorisches Museum, Vienna.

11 Max Kurzweil (1867–1916)
Death of the Dryad, c. 1898. Oil. Historisches Museum der Stadt Wien.

12 Albin Egger-Lienz (1868–1926)
The Cross, 1901. Oil. Museum Ferdinandeum, Innsbruck.

13 Kolomon Moser (1868–1918)
Poster for the Fifth Exhibition of the Vienna Secession, 1899. Color lithograph. Historisches Museum der Stadt Wien.

14 Kolomon Moser (1868–1918)
Loïe Fuller, c. 1900. Watercolor, india ink. Albertina, Vienna.

15 Gustav Klimt (1862–1918)
Love, 1895. Oil. Historisches Museum der Stadt Wien.

16 Gustav Klimt (1862–1918)
The Virgin, 1913. Oil. Narodni Galerie, Prague.

The
Fantastic
Art of
Vienna

AUSTRIA & HUNGARY

NOTE
Countries of the Austrian Crown..........
„   „ „ Hungarian „ ....
Territories acquired by Austria in 1908

ENGLISH MILES
0   50   100   150

KILOMETRES
0   50   100   150   200   250

Railways thus

Illus. 1. The Plague Monument
in Vienna's Graben, consecrated
1693. Photograph.

The Fantastic Art of Vienna

Long before the Viennese dreamt the dreams that would be probed with such startling consequences by Sigmund Freud, the city of Vienna had fabricated a fantasy concept of itself as realm of laughter and light. Even the rest of the world called it the City of Dreams. This beguiling image, mirrored in the city's lavish architectural self-portrait — the Ringstrasse — reflected a world of make-believe, in which the magnificent façades of imperial palace, museums, parliament, theater, and opera house attested to a dedication to spectacle and status quo. Right up to 1914 the city of Vienna presented the world with the most beautiful waltzes and the most stirring marches, while its painters, culminating with Gustav Klimt, dazzled the eye with bacchantic yet increasingly tragic icons of bizarre beauty.

The demonic origins of Vienna, too often glossed over by its historians although periodically articulated by its artists, sprang from a centuries-old flight from death. Capital of an empire that for a thousand years had been the easternmost outpost of Christendom against the Turks, Vienna was a very old cemetery in which the suffering of centuries lay interred. Underground labyrinths preserved the memories of invasions, massacres, fires, floods, and disastrous epidemics. Since the end

of the seventeenth century a marble obelisk adorned with writhing figures (Illus. 1), the Plague Monument (consecrated 1693), had brooded over the heart of downtown Vienna — the *Graben* (Graves) — as a macabre reminder of the Plague of 1679. Four years after the Plague a different pestilence threatened Vienna in the form of the dreaded Ottoman Turks. Amid the battle cries of "Allah" and "Jesus" resounding across a bloody Danube, the Moslem siege of the Christian stronghold came within a hair's-breadth of victory before a final rout was achieved. The melée served as a palpable reminder of the city's fantastic historical position: poised on the tightrope between Orient and Occident. The peculiarly excessive nature of Austrian Baroque art was fashioned in the euphoric aftermath of release from plague and siege at the end of the seventeenth century.

Escape from death encouraged flight from reality: melancholic merrymaking and a compelling make-believe became components of Vienna's periodic predilection for fantastic art and magic plays. Even the German language, as spoken in Vienna, came to reflect the tension of a fantastic existence. People and objects were approached and "tamed" with diminutives (*Mäderl* — young girl; *Häusel* — little house), and in a world of uncer-

3

tain action, "could" and "would" gave way to "should," so that by frequent use of the optative (Man möchte bitte hereintreten? — Should you please like to come in?) reality was wheedled, coddled, and clichéed into a friendly compliance with tentative wish-states.[1]

In the Austrian half of the Austro-Hungarian Empire the German language itself led a funambulistic existence as native tongue of only 35 percent of the entire population. The majority (60 percent) belonged to a Slav language bloc consisting of Czechs, Slovaks, Poles, Ruthenes, and South Slavs. Confronting different languages, different nations, and different directions at the same time had become the habitual as well as historical stance of the Habsburgs; in fact, the Habsburg family emblem was a two-headed eagle that, like the state, had simultaneously to look both east and west.

Just how pervasively the element of the fantastic was a daily fact of life in the thousand-year-old Habsburg Empire is reflected in the diverse races that made up the realm. At the brink of World War I, the Dual Monarchy numbered the following populations and nationalities:

> 0.6 million Islamic Slavs
> 0.8 million Italians
> 1.4 million Slovenes
> 2.0 million Slovaks
> 2.0 million Serbs
> 2.9 million Rumanians
> 3.2 million Croats
> 4.0 million Ruthenes
> 5.0 million Poles
> 6.6 million Czechs
> 10.0 million Hungarians
> 12.0 million Germans

These figures included two million Jews, the majority of whom — typified by the Galician rural Jew — were desperately poor, and whose right to own property and to vote had been granted only sixty-five years earlier. As for the small number of Jews who by their intellectual and artistic achievements figured so predominantly in the cultural life of increasingly anti-Semitic urban centers, Vienna, Budapest, and Prague, the composer Gustav Mahler summed up the bizarre paradox of being a Jewish "alien" in the Habsburg Empire: "I am thrice homeless. As a native of Bohemia in Austria, as an Austrian among Germans, and as a Jew throughout all the world. Everywhere an intruder, never welcomed."[2] The unsettling sensation of feeling an unwelcome stranger in one's homeland was a phenomenon affecting all ethnic groups in the Austro-Hungarian Empire, and was experienced by Italian, Slovak, Serb, Pole, Magyar, and Austrian alike. Stirred by some chimerical hand, the gigantic cauldron of potentially clashing races had been steaming to a boil for centuries, ever since 1526, the birth-year of the Dual Monarchy, when Bohemia, Moravia, Hungary, and Austria were united under a single crown.

From this miscegenetic union was born the fantastic art of Vienna. The two-headed eagle would henceforth gaze at two worlds: the real and the imaginary. The fantastic art of Vienna seems always to have oscillated between two pronounced concerns: exploration of nature and exposition of the self. The first subject — a mysterious world of elemental forces, sometimes hostile, sometimes poetically intoxicating — emerged in the same century as the founding of the Dual Monarchy, with the appearance of the Danube School. This group of painters addressed themselves with singular devotion to the romantic landscape accompanying the Danube on its course from the Black Forest through Bavaria and the North Austrian plain to Vienna. The leading representative of the School was the Bavarian-born Albrecht Altdorfer (ca. 1480 – 1538), who made two extended visits to Vienna, in 1510 – 11 and again in 1535, where he painted several religious works. It was in the intimacy of his chiaroscuro brush drawings, however, that Altdorfer best demonstrated his sense of the drama of nature's secret forces. In the pen and chalk drawing The Wild People of the Woods (Black and White Plate 1), for example, the agitation of the human characters is paralleled by an animistic plant world which trembles and sways toward the figures, suggesting a mystical bond between nature and humans. Murder has been committed in the forest, and the primeval witnesses shudder silently.

Exploration of an anthropomorphic nature is one aspect of Viennese fantastic art; exposition of the self has played an even more dominant role. One of the earliest and most engaging presentations of the self by an artist working in Vienna is the carved Self-Portrait of the Sculptor (Black and White Plate 2) of about 1515 at the base of the magnificent Four Church Fathers pulpit created by Anton Pilgram (ca. 1460 – ca. 1515) for St. Stephen's Cathedral.[3] "Master Antoni" of the nearby town of Brno is documented as coming to Vienna to take the position of master of works for the cathedral in 1511. Snakes and toads writhe up the rail of the pulpit's sculpted balustrade toward the four church fathers, vying in their slithering realism with the delightful trompe l'oeil effect achieved by the sculptor in his own carved effigy. He shows himself bust-length, emerging from an interior and leaning with his right elbow and forearm on a window sill, while with his left hand he pulls open a window. Although his eyes are left blank, without carved pupils, the sculptor's gaze is fixed in a ruminative downward look. An earnest sense of self as artist (he holds a compass in his right hand) is the final impression conveyed by this curious and unforgettable "window gazer" (Fenstergucker) who, in an age of anonymous artisans, did not hesitate to introduce his very secular self into a building dedicated to the divine.

The artist *as* artist was an important aspect of self-exposition in Vienna during the next two centuries. This would seem quite natural, as the role of the artist in society changed from the anonymity of late Gothic and early Renaissance times to the prestige and financial security of court appointments in the Baroque period. Nevertheless, a predilection for the *unusual* and slightly fantastic self-portrait — be it in the quality of intensity or in the juggleries of color — was evinced long before the modern period of narcissistic self-display by the late Baroque artist Franz Anton Maulbertsch (1724 – 1796). His "artist *as* artist" *Self-Portrait* (Black and White Plate 3) is extraordinary — not in its overt motif, but in its glowering, mysterious mood, which, the longer one looks, seems increasingly to dominate the canvas with its threat of coloristic fulmination. Argent and murky at the same time, simultaneously dazzling and hazy, Maulbertsch's eerie palette robs objects of their corporeality and hints at an invisible nervous system of seething energy. Like an Austrian El Greco, Maulbertsch elongates his figure and environment and endows himself with flamelike fingers of enormous size and glittering vitality. He wears a flowing fur-trimmed frock coat, symbol of professional success, and yet his expression is rigid and tense. The painter's right eye makes defiant contact with the beholder while the left eye wanders to one side in the traditional attitude of introspection. A pronounced and unsettling subjectivity pervades this strange presentation of self. The pose is grandiose, expansive, expository — he displays one of his own portrait studies, perhaps an early self-portrait — and secure; the flapping strands of environment are marginal and distracting, however, and the area around the artist's isolated head is inexplicably a void. Unseen tensions are producing felt emotions; the composition is correspondingly agitated, and a furious brushstroke imparts an expressionistic furor to the whole. Maulbertsch imparted this same sense of the fantastic to his ambitious religious and historical frescoes as well, and his flickering compositions and eccentric use of color optics not only contribute to the demonic element of late Baroque, from which Goya was to spring, but also anticipate the painterly writhings of Kokoschka and other Viennese Expressionist artists. With Maulbertsch's late *Self-Portrait*, an irreversible subjectivity was inculcated into the fantastic aspect of Viennese self-depiction.

The most fantastic self-scrutiny of the century, however — perhaps of the whole Age of Enlightenment — was the bizarre autoscopy practiced by the sculptor Franz Xaver Messerschmidt (1736 – 1783). Chronologically he appeared as two separate personalities: the successful portrait sculptor of Empress Maria Theresia and her court and, after 1774, the bitter recluse subject to delusions of persecution and hellbent on carving a gallery of Doppelgängers as depositories for his fleeting and violently disturbed moods (Black and White Plates 4a – d, 5). His early years seemed charmed and held no hint of the psychic illness to come. As a boy he was apprenticed to his two sculptor uncles, Johann and Philipp Jakob Staub, first in Munich and then in Graz. At sixteen he was accepted as a student at the Vienna Academy where the director took a personal interest in him and eventually obtained a place for him with the Imperial Armory as a metal founder. A productive trip to Rome in 1765 and a decade of sculpting the likenesses of the Viennese aristocracy made him the favorite of the imperial court, and he was appointed assistant professor of sculpture at the Vienna Academy in 1769. Two years later, at the age of thirty-five, Messerschmidt suffered a mysterious "confusion in the head," from which he recovered enough to go on sculpting but not enough to continue as an effective teacher. Such was the opinion of the Austrian prime minister, Count von Kaunitz, who, upon the death of the ranking professor of sculpture at the Academy in 1774, explained to the Empress why her favorite sculptor had not been recommended as successor by his colleagues:

... for three years [Messerschmidt] has shown signs of some confusion ... that confusion in his head ... is still evident in a not perfectly healthy imagination ... he believes all other professors and directors to be his enemies: he still has odd and peculiar whims.... [4]

As was the case with his almost exact contemporary, the "wizard" advocate of animal magnetism Franz Anton Mesmer (1734 – 1815), who during the years 1759 – 1777 also experienced rejection by his Viennese colleagues, Messerschmidt could never forget the rebuff. He ascribed this setback in his career to professional envy and haughtily refused the pension offered by the concerned Empress. He quit Vienna for Munich, where he bombarded and dismayed prospective patrons with horror stories of his Viennese "enemies." By 1777, believing that "all Germany feels obliged to persecute me," he took refuge with a brother who lived in Pressburg on the Danube (Bratislava in present-day Czechoslovakia), some thirty miles east of his now-hated Vienna. Here his eccentricity took full hold. Coveting solitude, he bought a house in an eerie, rundown district near the Jewish cemetery, and in an austere workshop almost devoid of furnishings, Messerschmidt confronted his "enemies." They were himself. Every one of the sixty-nine nearly life-size lead or marble busts (Black and White Plates 4 a-d and 5) which the artist produced during those years was based on his own face. The busts vary in range of distortion from clearly recognizable self-portraits with fixed, empty expressions and changing hairlines, to spasmodic grimacers with furrowed brows, wrinkled noses, and bulging or slit eyes. Many of the heads share a repeated feature — tightly closed lips — giving the effect of

5

incredible pressure. Messerschmidt had his own explanation for the "Egyptian," or "character," heads, as they came to be known after his death. The Berlin bookseller and travel writer Friedrich Nicolai won the lonely sculptor's confidence on a visit to his Pressburg hideaway in 1781, and was actually allowed to watch the artist at work. Messerschmidt followed a strange and uncanny procedure: working in front of a mirror to which he made frequent reference, he would inflict a mighty pinch to the side of his body just below the ribs, react with a frightening facial expression, and study the frozen countenance in the mirror. He would sculpt assiduously for a few minutes and then resume the grimace for further concentrated examination. Intrigued, Nicolai persuaded the sculptor to explain his astonishing actions, and the hermit-artist embarked upon a jumbled narrative from which a familiar pattern of persecution emerged. Now it was not the Academy professors but the "demons of proportions" who envied Messerschmidt his near-perfect artistic talents. The demons bothered him "particularly at night," causing him pain in the stomach and thighs—this in spite of the "chaste life" he had lived since his youth! The pinching ordeal was Messerschmidt's way of expelling the demons. He had "discovered" that use of an ancient Egyptian system of universal and analogous proportions could stave off the demons' onslaughts and at the same time bring him closer to the secret of perfect proportions. Messerschmidt's heavy-handed pinching thwarted his torturers and even allowed him to portray the chief demon in two, smaller marble busts, one with eyes bulging, the other with eyes squinted shut. Such drastic exorcism compensated for the imprisoned passions that held Messerschmidt in their grip and that struggled to erupt through the tightly sealed lips of his Doppelgänger heads.

Messerschmidt's "possession" by persecuting demons and his pseudo-scientific "solution"— fantastic as it may seem to the modern mind— were not incongruous with the spirit of the eighteenth century, that age of reason which abounded in charlatans, sorcerers, faith healers, physiognomists, occultists, animists, fluidists, hypnotists, and spiritualists from Casanova and Cagliostro to Lavater and Mesmer. Mozart himself responded to the topicality of animal magnetism in the Vienna of 1790 by poking gentle fun at the family friend, Herr von Mesmer, in Così fan tutte. In the famous magnet finale of the opera's first act, Despina is given a great "Mesmer stone" with the power of drawing poison from the body.

This playful reference to Mesmerism is not the only tribute to the world of invisible forces and fantasy in Mozart's work. In Don Giovanni (1787) the awesome ghost of the Commendatore hounds the unrepentant seducer of his daughter to eternal damnation, and the extravagant fairy-tale setting of The Magic Flute (1791) so pleased the Viennese public

that a hunger for more "magic" plays became the overriding passion of an entire new generation of opera- and theater-goers. The beginning of the nineteenth century saw this appetite for Zauberpossen (magic farces) nourished by Vienna's great actor-playwrights, the tenderly humorous Ferdinand Raimund (1790–1836) and the bitterly sarcastic Johannes Nestroy (1802–1882).

The opening years of the nineteenth century in Vienna also saw military invasions of the city by the French. By 1812 the cosmopolitan capital on the Danube had attracted some of the leading voices of the Romantic Movement—that new European sensibility born under the impact of Napoleon's self-propelled rise from obscurity to threatened world domination. As a result of the Napoleonic invasions of Austria a heightened awareness of national heritage, common linguistic identity, and political mission permeated the writings of the German Romantics clustered in Vienna. And it was in literature rather than in the visual arts that the components of Romanticism best suited for fantastic imagery first appeared. Among the writers in Vienna in the year 1812 were Joseph von Eichendorff, whose restless, melancholy lyrics addressed a permanently moonlit nature, Clemens Brentano, passionate collector of German folk songs, Ludwig Tieck, whose writings glorified the Middle Ages, Karl Theodor Körner, whose heroic death as a freedom fighter the following year brought his patriotic poems to posthumous fame, and the mentally unbalanced poet-turned-orator-priest Zacharias Werner, whose fascination by the abnormal and probings into religious psychology and sexual intoxication anticipated Freud.

The presence of the Schlegel brothers in Vienna lent tremendous authority to Romanticism's reverence for the art of the past. August Schlegel's celebrated lectures during the winter of 1807—8 (published 1809—11) single-handedly introduced the notion of aesthetic relativism: Vienna's gothic St. Stephen's Cathedral was cited as different from but equal in artistic merit to the Pantheon, with the admonishment: "Does our admiration of the one compel us to depreciate the other?" Friedrich Schlegel's Vienna University lectures of 1812 reinforced this influential judgment and again drew attention to the artistic and architectural glories of the German Middle Ages—a sentiment well geared to the burgeoning nationalism that for the rest of the century would sentimentally associate the Gothic with a German genius (See Color Plate 4).

But it was not just the remembrance of things past that Napoleon's two triumphal entries into Vienna triggered. Military humiliation, which the city experienced in 1805 and again in 1809, reinforced the deep-seated Viennese craving for distraction from the world of reality. As Austrian corpses floated down the Danube during the fateful summer of 1809, the Viennese threw themselves with feral intensity into the popular craze for dancing. For a century to come, release into the fantasy world for the average citizen would be accomplished not so much through art as through music and the waltz. Mozart's friend, the Irish tenor Michael O'Kelly, wrote with amazement in his memoirs about the dance mania he had witnessed in Vienna (1786) and the "continuous frenzy" of the waltzing that lasted "from 10 o'clock at night till 7 o'clock in the morning," with a special lying-in room provided for pregnant women who insisted upon three-four rotation right up to delivery. Like a spinning top the population of Vienna whirled away its worries at the Apollo Palace. This magnificent dance hall, opened as a shrewd commercial investment and gesture of patriotism in 1808 by the orthopedic surgeon Sigmund Wolffsohn, who had amassed a fortune through his manufacture of movable artificial limbs, provided a fantastic dream empire, with architectural decorations ranging from Turkish to Greek, where the Viennese could forget their defeats in the dance. Rival dance pavilions sprang up all over the city and, while the august members of the Congress of Vienna rearranged Napoleon's Empire during the day, they waltzed by night. (The Prince von Ligne observed: "Congrès ne marche pas, il danse.") The dance mania became a narcotic, and by 1830 the former French emperor's domain was preempted by a Viennese music monarch, Johann Strauss.

The writer Heinrich Laube, who came to Vienna in 1833, recognized this phenomenon and gave the following analysis of the waltz king at work (Illus. 2):

In the middle of the [Sperl] garden on the orchestra platform there stands the modern hero of Austria, *le Napoléon autrichien,* the musical director Johann Strauss. The Strauss waltzes are to the Viennese what the Napoleonic victories were to the French.... I was very curious to see the Austrian Napoleon and it pleased me to find him in the center of the battlefield. He was just fighting his Austerlitz as we arrived. With his bow he was pointing to the heavens and the violins were acclaiming

Illus. 2. Johann Strauss Sr. conducting at the Sperl, 1830. Lithograph.

the rising of the sun. There he stood before me, the third of the triumvirate of which Napoleon is the first and Paganini the second.... All eyes were turned to him; it was a moment of worship....What does he look like, this Johann Strauss? If Napoleon's appearance was classically Roman and calmly antique, if Paganini's was romantic and arresting as moonlight, so that of Maestro Strauss is African and hot-blooded, crazy from the sun, modern, bold, fidgety, restless, unbeautiful, passionate.... Typically African too is the way he conducts his dances; his own limbs no longer belong to him when the desert-storm of his waltz is let loose; his fiddle-bow dances with his arms; the tempo animates his feet; the melody waves champagne glasses in his face....The devil is abroad.... The power wielded by the black-haired musician is potentially very dangerous; it is his especial good fortune that no censorship can be exercised over waltz music and the thoughts or emotions it arouses....He is a man who could do a great deal of harm if he were to play Rousseau's ideas on his violin.[5]

The total abandonment of the waltzers was also noted by Laube:

And now begin the preparations for the real dancing. To keep the unruly crowds back, a long rope is put up and all who remain in the center of the hall are separated from the actual dancers. The boundary, however, is fluctuating and flexible; it is only possible to distinguish the dancers by watching the girls' heads in steady rotation. The couples waltz straight through any accidental hindrances in their joyful frenzy; no god holds them back, not even the intense heat which is carried backwards and forwards in penetrating waves, as if driven by African desert winds.... These orgies last till the early morning...the waltzes stir the blood like the bite of a tarantula.[6]

Viennese escapism was thus set to music and acquired an intoxicating three-quarter rhythm. The Romantics gave their enthusiastic approval to this activity which, like the mathematical symbol for infinity, wound back upon itself with no true beginning or end and gave its participants the heady sensation of being lost in space. A nation that under Metternich was not allowed to express itself politically found its fantasy release in the dance.

The repressive era of Prince von Metternich (1773–1859) engendered an aesthetic escapism and personal resignation in the average citizen — *der kleine Mann* — of the Austro-Hungarian Empire, who took his fate with good-humored grumbling and who became the new folk hero of stage and song. This widespread and petty cultural attitude in the age of political reactionism and multiplying bureaucracy came to be summed up in the epithet "Biedermeier." This was the name of a fictitious village schoolmaster, Gottlieb Biedermeier, of popular literature, who placed a premium on orderliness above sense, routine over rebellion, and pious performance of duty over critical reflection. Stirred only by the rhythm of the waltz, the Biedermeier man of passivity and political indifference now replaced the fiery poet-soldier of Napoleonic times. Reverie, not action, was the opiate of the mid-nineteenth-century Austrian. The Viennese dramatist Franz Grillparzer (1791–1872) created what might be called a Biedermeier Faust in his *Der Traum ein Leben* (*The Dream, a Life*, 1834), in which Rustan, the Austrian hero, merely *dreams* that he embarks on heroic deeds. Such substitution of illusion for reality was more than a literary theme; it became a national pastime. With all the world as a stage, the Viennese acted out their humdrum lives with self-conscious exhibitionism, carping at fate with impeccable manners. If, through its sensuous celebration of waltz, wine, and flirtation, Vienna was well on its way to becoming the fabled City of Dreams, so through its fanatical insistence on the "correctness" of conduct and social appearances, the capital was also drawing that much closer to the inflexible façade that would ultimately stifle and paralyze an entire nation.

No part was better suited to support the make-believe universe of Biedermeier propriety than the visual arts. Every citizen could satisfy an individual desire for immortality, and sharp, close-focus line portraiture became commonplace. The photographic verisimilitude of Vienna's great portrait painter Ferdinand Georg Waldmüller (1793–1865) exhibits a pursuit of reality that is almost demonic in its rapacious intensity. The dazzling virtuosity of this Austrian Ingres, whose motto was "back to nature," especially welcomed the painterly challenge of reproducing light—usually a hard, direct sunlight that bathes objects with a glittering, almost magical clarity. Occasionally Waldmüller's keenness for corporeal presence as defined by light led him to reject the Biedermeier matter-of-factness for the drama of the unusual. Such a picture is his *Roman Ruins in Schönbrunn Castle Park* (Black and White Plate 6). The architectural spectacle had been built as a romantic ruin in 1778, and for the observant painter it served as a marvelous depository for the elusive, deep pockets of light that were reflected by the translucent water of a still pool onto the jumble of undergrowth, statues, and architectural fragments. The dreamlike super-reality found in so many of Waldmüller's landscapes, frequently with an exaggeratedly low or high horizon line (a feature not lost on Klimt), can also animate his portraiture. The *Boy With Lantern* (Color Plate 1) is a tour de force study of the startlingly theatrical effects obtainable by the unusual placement of an artificial light. Waldmüller's precision of form enhances the spectral qualities of the suddenly revealed image—a mischievous phantasm in an age of realism.

Such casting of the familiar into an unusual context was part of the success of Moritz von Schwind

Illus. 3. Schubert and his friends Schwind and Vogel serenading while Vienna sleeps, 1862, by Moritz von Schwind from the "Lachner Roll."

(1804–1871), the century's most prolific spinner of fairy tales and fantasy. Although he left his unappreciative native Vienna at the age of thirty-five, his early experiences there stamped his character and his art for life. When he was nineteen he met Franz Schubert, six years his senior and equally disregarded by Vienna. Soon the two were inseparable and the Schubert circle moved their merry games and musical activities to the Schwind family property—a rural oasis in the center of Vienna with a garden courtyard and an unbroken view of the Wiener Wald. The main building was known as the Moonshine House, and it was here that the Schubertians serenaded while Vienna slept (Illus. 3). Schwind and Schubert were of such similar temperament, with a natural gaiety fissured by fits of gloom, that Schubert jestingly called the painter his sweetheart, and Schwind declared: "As Schubert composes, so do I paint." And indeed the fluidity of Schwind's draftsmanship suggests an analogy with the lyricism of Schubert's musical line. The painter and composer in one instance treated the same subject, Goethe's spooky ballad, *The Erl King*. Schubert's musical setting was jotted down in a few hours on the last day of December 1815; Schwind's macabre representation (Black and White Plate 7) dates from around 1830, and shows the artist's early fascination by primeval forest scenes—an attraction kindled not so much by the earlier example of Altdorfer and the Danube School as by real life and the year he spent as a young boy with an uncle whose home was in the romantic Bohemian Forest (Altgedein). The impressions of great expanses of unexplored wildwood provided Schwind with a lifelong supply of imaginary forest retreats into which to drop his never-ending dramatis personae of elves (Color Plate 2), gnomes, hermits, saints, wandering knights, lost princesses, wild horses, water spirits, and wood sprites. In spite of eventual professional success, Schwind's later years found the melancholic tendency of his youth exacerbated by lack of recognition. His great cyclic scenes of legends, folk songs, and fairy tales continued to favor a morose, supernatural element (Color Plate 3), while he ironically referred to himself as "already stricken from the roll of living artists." One of the most winsome of this modern minnesinger's fantasies is *Erwin von Steinbach's Dream* (Color Plate 4). Erwin, the medieval architect of Strassburg minster, elevated to a hero's pedestal by Goethe in his essay glorifying German gothic architecture (*Von deutscher Baukunst*, 1772), is accompanied by a solicitous angel on a floating tour of the interior of a great cathedral. (Schwind does not show Strassburg but Vienna's own St. Stephen's Cathedral.) Thus Goethe's *Sturm und Drang* fantasy became a nineteenth-century Romantic dream with repercussions in the real world, as the drive to complete unfinished cathedrals swept all German-speaking peoples with nationalistic fervor.

In the City of Dreams itself, the favorite mid-century pastime was not architectural exertion but romantic spectacle. This was available quite handily at the local *Kärntnertortheater* where, ever since 1837 Fanny Elssler (1810–1884) had regularly returned to her hometown to star in the ballet extravaganzas that had made her the world famous rival of Maria Taglioni. The age of "pure ocular spectacle" as an art form separate from opera had arrived. The new ballet featured devices dear to the heart of Romanticism: exotic and mysterious scenes set in magic forests or haunted palaces, diorama effects simulating tempests and sunsets, complicated plots drawn from literature and set to music by first-rate composers. Graceful female performers seemed actually to float — thanks to the recent introduction of pointe work. Elssler starred in many of the greatest Romantic ballets: *The Fairy and the Knight*, *La Sylphide*, *La Gipsy* [sic], *La Tarentule*, *Giselle*, and *La Esmeralda*, captivating audiences not only in Vienna but in Paris, London, Berlin, St. Petersburg, and in American cities as well. However, it was the 1843 divertisement *The Painter's Dream Picture* (*Des Malers Traumbild*[7]) that answered most directly the Viennese demand for fantasy. The dance was supposedly based on a real event in the life of a painter who fell in love with a ballerina, painted her portrait, and promptly became so obsessed with the painted image that he neglected the real dancer. The plot thus presented an updating of the Pygmalion-Galatea story, and the breathlessly awaited dénouement showed a jealous Fanny Elssler as the "real" ballerina, nimbly stepping out of the picture's frame to expel her painted image

Illus. 4. Fanny Elssler in the ballet divertissement *The Painter's Dream Picture*, 1843.

once and for all from the mind of her amazed lover (Illus. 4). Reality triumphing over fantasy? Not in Vienna. The "dream picture" ballet became synonymous with wish-fulfillment. Rapt contemplation of the imaginary could produce the real thing — a characteristic Viennese twist on Schopenhauer's aesthetic escapism, and fodder for the Freudian psychoanalysis awaiting its cue offstage in the wings of time.

Ballet, theater, opera, and the waltz; taken in weekly doses these habit-forming stimulants provided a magical alternative to the Biedermeier routine of life in Alt Wien (Old Vienna). But what of the painters themselves? Did they create their own extravaganzas, and were pictures of exotic themes and places in demand by the public? The answer — in a Biedermeier epoch — is no. Painting in Vienna during the late 1830s to the early 1860s was the most conservative of the arts. With the exception of individual late Romantics like Schwind, contemporary painters were not inclined toward fantasy. Instead these artists took upon themselves the task of recording, often with maudlin sentimentality, the events of daily life in comfortable, cozy, cluttered Alt Wien. Live and let live — Metternich's reactionism had reached the fine arts. Social genre painting — animation without agitation — became the mirror that Vienna held up to reflect an existence no longer threatened by pestilence or external politics.

Nevertheless, even among the journalistically minded genre painters, there was at least one sharp-eyed reporter who occasionally espied and depicted a rent in the social fabric. This was Josef Danhauser (1805–1845), the "Englishman" of his day; Hogarth's cynical eighteenth-century chronicles of the hypocrisies of society inspired Danhauser to treat similar themes (*The Spendthrift*, 1836; *The Eye Doctor*, 1837; *The Opening of the Will*, 1839). Such gentle mockery provoked the displeasure of art critics, who in turn became the objects of Danhauser's scorn in an amusing fantasy, *The Art Critics* (*Dog Comedy*) (Black and White Plate 8). The picture shows the bedlam in the studio of an artist who has fallen asleep in his armchair, oblivious of an invasion by three belligerent dogs who knock over papers, tea cup, and ink pot and single out drawings for canine destruction. Atop the clutter of the desk crouches an especially pugnacious pug, whose features, in a Vienna of 1841, were instantly recognizable as those of the self-appointed art critic Moritz Saphir (1795–1853), editor of the *Humorist*, in whose pages the work of Danhauser had been described as "moral haranguing" (*Moralpaukerei*). The painting's message was clear: the venomous spilt ink of the critic has sullied the work of the painter. With this whimsical self-defense Danhauser initiated an art of painterly rebuttal that was picked up with relish by later Viennese artists who also had scores to settle with hostile critics. Thus Klimt would paint the perfect, if inescapably scatological, response to his critics with his *Goldfish* of 1901–2 (originally titled *To My Critics*), in which a naked woman, seen from below, very deliberately directs her callipygian rebuttal at the beholder-critic. A few years later Arnold Schönberg would take out his indignation at the ridicule of his music by painting ghoulish "portraits" of imaginary critics with enormous, but deaf ears(Illus. 16).

Just as Danhauser provided occasional startling glimpses into the mores of city life, so August von Pettenkofen (1822–1889) frequently caught the unconventional and picturesque quality of life in the rural areas of the Austro-Hungarian Empire. His early works treated military subjects on barren battlefields; later he discovered the inhabitants of the open plains, especially the East Hungarian Puzta villagers around Szolnok, where from 1851 on he visited regularly. Hungary, for an Austrian in search of the exotic, was far more mysterious than Italy or Spain. With increasingly impressionistic smears and broken tones, Pettenkofen evoked the piquant atmosphere, romantic horse-training, and somewhat fatalistic mood of Hungarian rural life. He was especially fascinated by the "sinister" gypsies, who lived their proudly separate lives as nomads, and one of his most dramatic pictures deals sympathetically with what his Hungarian peasant friends would have considered a daily occurrence, *Gypsy Thief Chased by Dogs* (Black and White Plate 9).

Gypsies! Those mysterious roving peoples of Europe who startled the Congress of Vienna by their mere existence and who would later claim Hitler's relentless attention in his drive to "purify" the German race. They constituted one of the most fantastic elements of the Austro-Hungarian Empire. Fanny Elssler had scored a triumph with her ballet *La Gipsy* of 1839; Liszt had elevated the alien music of the gypsy to a revolutionary component of Hungarian nationalism with his "Hungarian Rhapsodies" of 1840. In the spring of 1853 Brahms succumbed to the *bacillus hungaricus*, infected by the flashy Hungarian gypsy violinist, Eduard Reményi, who persuaded the sober North German to be his accompanist on a spur-of-the-moment concert tour. And in 1885 Johann Strauss, Jr. proclaimed a reconciliation between the Hungarian and Austrian halves of the Empire with his fabulously successful operetta *Zigeunerbaron* (*Gypsy Baron*). A gypsy fantasia replaced the waltz mania as Vienna discovered one more outlet for her suppressed dreams.

The Biedermeier calm that had lulled Viennese senses during the 1850s was broken in the second half of the century by a strange new restlessness which first appeared in the astonishing work of Anton Romako (1832–1889). Like Messerschmidt, the Vienna-born Romako experienced initial success as an artist but suffered a subsequent alienation from society that left him a bitter and forgotten recluse. In a sixteen-page autobiographical fragment[8] the artist proudly identified himself as painter of "history, portraits, etc." and recalled the days of his youth, before the advent of railroads, when he had traveled through Germany, Italy, and Spain by wagon, horse and mule, seeing his first gypsies in the forest outside Munich. Early art studies in Vienna and Munich were followed by a financially rewarding nineteen-year residence in Rome (1857–1876), where with virtuoso rapidity he perfected a popular genre and portrait style. In his works two different trends evolved: a translation of environment into agitated paint surfaces (Color Plate 5), anticipating the *horror vacuii* of Klimt's solidified decorative surrounds; and an individual concentration on the subject against an empty background (Color Plate 6), forecasting the Expressionist voids of Gerstl, Kokoschka, and Schiele. Back in Vienna Romako produced an unusual series of pure landscapes, including several views of the Gastein valley (1877), of which the most haunting is the night scene *The Hot Springs of Gastein in Festival Illumination* (Color Plate 5), with its curious natural and artificial light phenomena.

The luminosity of this glowing night piece explodes with the full blinding force of noon in Romako's bizarre "history" piece *Admiral Tegetthoff in the Sea Battle at Lissa* (Color Plate 6). Like a latter-day Austrian Géricault, Romako selected a recent drama at sea for his subject. Rear Admiral Baron Wilhelm von Tegetthoff (Illus. 5 and 6) had figured in the dramatic Austro-Italian naval battle off the Austrian-held island of Lissa on 20 July 1866. A large Italian fleet had bombarded the island fortifications and Tegetthoff, with a command of only eight ships, had steamed to the rescue. His flagship was the *Archduke Ferdinand Max*, built after plans by Romako's older brother Josef, a marine engineer. Upon sighting the larger Italian fleet, Tegetthoff hoisted the signals: CLOSE IN—FULL SPEED—IRONCLADS, CHARGE THE ENEMY AND RAM![9] It was not a precise rendering of the superstructure of his brother's ship that interested Romako the painter, but rather the drama of the actual moment when Tegetthoff's frigate rammed its enemy, the Italian cruiser *Re d'Italia*. Exploding light and human crisis are the true subjects of this strange painting. The picture is divided into two tiers with nine uni-

Illus. 5. Rear Admiral Wilhelm von Tegetthoff, 1864. Photograph.

Illus. 6. Rear Admiral Wilhelm von Tegetthoff with his crew, 1864. Photograph.

formed figures silhouetted against a bright, flashing background. In the lower half of the picture five Austrian sailors grimly hold the great steering wheel on collision course, while above them on the command bridge three officers flank their commander in varying poses of apprehension. The admiral, his hands thrust in his pockets and his legs braced wide apart, stands motionless. The sailors on the lower deck seem already to be reeling from the crash: their active shapes create a pyramid that mounts from a base of resoluteness through horror to an apex of defiance, expressed in the center figure's heroic waving of his cap in the face of the Italian ship. Just the opposite of heroics is expressed by the seemingly casual stance of Tegetthoff, directly above the cap-waving sailor. "A drastic caricature," complained the Viennese press. And yet for those who could accept the novelty of Romako's stacked composition and detail-obliterating light, it was Tegetthoff's fixed stare that gave this action picture its unique and literal impact. The incongruous calm of this mesmerized and mesmerizing commander amid the storm of battle produced a fantastic super-reality which the beholder — who occupies the place of the enemy ship — still must experience today.

Romako's obstinate pictorial "strangeness" and the tragic events of his personal life — his two teen-age daughters took their lives in a romantic suicide pact with a young Italian architect — led to the rumor that Romako too died by his own hand.

Although the painter died a natural death from sudden kidney failure, the popular theory of suicide became so widespread that almost a quarter of a century later Egon Schiele sympathetically referred to Romako's being driven to suicide.[10] It is interesting that an Expressionist artist such as Schiele would cite Romako's supposed fate. Romako's eerie pictures, with their dramatic break from the mainstream of Biedermeier realism, formed a spiritual bond between the bravura fantasies of Austrian Baroque painting and the psychological hallucinations of Viennese Expressionism.

Romako and his ungainly style were stubbornly out of step with his times, but the elegant Hans Makart (1840–1884) — eight years his junior — was destined to become the impresario of a lush pictorial ensemble that would become the rage, in fact the passion, of Vienna. The secret of Makart's success was the grafting of an old style — realism — on to new content — exotica. Vienna's latest escapism was introduced in the guise of stereographic history painting: *The Plague in Florence* (1868), a three-panel eschatological orgy designed to be set among luxurious plants and water basins. This three-ring circus of thrashing bodies set against a "syphilitic background" (Moritz von Schwind) with its *Après nous le déluge* abandon became an overnight sensation upon its unveiling in Munich, where the young Austrian artist had trained under the history painter Carl Piloty. Such unabashed eroticism loom-

Illus. 7. Eduard Charlemont, *Hans Makart in His Atelier*, 1880. Oil.

ing so close to the surface of the "legitimate" exoticism of history painting was something Vienna had to have, and in fact a Viennese art dealer immediately purchased the panels. Influential admirers of Makart got the ear of the imperial court, and in April 1869 Kaiser Franz Josef himself invited Makart to set up house and atelier in Vienna in a spacious building (a former cannon foundry) near the Karlskirche, with all expenses paid. The painter accepted, and Bavaria's mad king, Ludwig II, lost a potential decorator for his dream castles. Makart took with him to Vienna his flair for erotic fantasy and infected that city with a strain of venereal virus from which in a sense it has never recovered. Imitating his good friend and admirer Richard Wagner, he pelted the citizenry with sensual imagery, orchestrated in overwhelmingly lavish color and articulated with insistent realism.

New "historical" icons such as *The Death of Cleopatra* (Color Plate 7) oozed from Makart's Venetian-Rubensian brush in what jealous detractors described as unstoppable "diarrheal productivity" (Anselm Feuerbach). Makart's studio (Illus. 7) was the source for the accoutrements of Vienna's new taste: giant palm fronds, polar bear and Persian rugs, Gobelin and oriental tapestries, velvet drapes, porcelain urns, bronze, terracotta, and marble statues, inlaid and carved furniture, mandolins,

mummies, antlers, oleander trees, suits of armor, columns, chandeliers, stuffed birds, and baldachinos. Not since the Apollo Palace had Vienna — city of dreams — possessed such a totally sensual dream world as Makart's exotic atelier (Color Plate 8). His sumptuous studio became a mandatory tourist stop for such well-known visitors to Vienna as Sarah Bernhardt. This state-supported fantasy was open to the public daily from four to five in the afternoon!

The theatricality of Makart's life (there were annual costume parties, including one in honor of Richard Wagner) and painting styles was well suited to the supreme effort asked of him by his adopted city in 1879. This was to take charge of the historical pageant for a city-wide celebration of the Kaiser's silver wedding anniversary. With gusto Makart threw himself into the task, designing three thousand costumes and thirty floats and selecting as his stylistic inspiration the German Renaissance. Some of his costumes were taken directly from the famous 137-piece woodcut cycle produced (more than three centuries earlier) by Hans Burgkmair, Albrecht Dürer, and others in the form of a triumphal procession for the Emperor Maximilian I. Makart himself dressed for the parade not as Dürer but as Rubens, thus signifying his and the city's perception of himself as an international painter-prince. Almost one million spectators from all corners of the Dual Monarchy watched the five-hour "living painting" of fourteen thousand persons proceed in a collective national fantasy along the Ringstrasse and past the Kaiser's tent. With his "Meistersinger" recreation of a Teutonic past (in which floats devoted to the steamboat and the railroad were not considered at all anachronistic), Makart proved himself to be the Wagner of the art world, and no one admired him more for this than Wagner himself.

Makart's mania for historical accuracy, as demonstrated in the pageant, found an excellent helpmate in photography, and he made extensive use of the medium, not only for his many successful society portraits but also for such historical portraits as *Cleopatra* or *Messalina*. His favorite photographic model was the popular Hofburgtheater actress Charlotte Wolter (1834–1897), the lascivious Messalina of Adolf Wilbrandt's recent stage success, who obligingly posed for the camera amid Makartian props (Illus. 8; compare Color Plate 7). The painter also turned the eye of the camera upon himself in a humorous self-portrait photomontage in which he appears ten times either as portrayer or as portrayed (Illus. 9).

The success of the protean creator of the "Makart Style" of sensual historicism was cut short. Within five years of the great pageant Makart was dead — a victim at the age of forty-four of syphilis. A bereft Vienna honored its prince of fantasy with a funeral procession that almost rivaled in pomp Makart's own epic pageant.

Erotica through exotica: this was the unsettling legacy that Makart bestowed upon his artistic heirs. Permissible guises for sensual fantasies: these were the allegorical and historical images that the Makart rage had sanctioned. Small wonder that Vienna's next generation came face to face with sexuality. Such direct confrontation produced two responses: Gustav Klimt (1862–1918) spent a lifetime veiling a naked Eros; Sigmund Freud (1856–1939) devoted all his efforts to uncovering the human libido.

But whether the cognitive process was to obscure or to reveal, the subject matter itself—sexuality—was already tainted by nineteenth-century concepts and mores. The age-old division between body and soul, recently reidentified by Nietzsche as Apollonian reason versus Dionysian passion, had equated man with intellect and woman with sensuality. By the end of the nineteenth century, not just Vienna but all literate Europe had adopted and paid fascinated homage to the concept of the *femme fatale*. From August Strindberg to the early Richard Strauss, the image of woman was to be defined as synonymous with greedy, mindless, uncontrolled, all-consuming sensuality.

Makart had resuscitated courtesans of the past, but the contemporary *femme fatale*—whose power would interest both Klimt and Freud—was dramatically introduced to the Viennese by yet another subject of the Austro-Hungarian Empire, the dour, enigmatic South Tyrolean painter of rural mountain life Giovanni Segantini (1858–1899). The austere work which so seized Viennese sensibilities that it was acquired for the Belvedere in 1901 was titled emphatically by the painter *The Evil Mothers* (Color Plate 9). The subject was a grim one, infanticide. Set against a vast Alpine expanse of snow-capped ridges, the writhing figure of a woman is seen impaled upon a lone tree, her face in an ecstasy of torment. As she literally and allegorically becomes a rotting branch, the life she has denied expires at her breast. The bloated face of her unwanted child is blue, its eyes closed in death (Color Plate 10). The terrible punishment inflicted upon this "wicked" mother does not seem to alter the way of womankind, however, for in the far left background a relentless procession of red-haired—that is, extra-sensual—"mothers" winds its way somnambulistically toward the same fate, while a tendrillike fetus crawls across the snow. Segantini's weird and wildly original picture was an unequivocal indictment of irresponsible self-gratification. It was rendered in rough mountain idiom with a directness to which the Viennese, with their habitual euphemization, were totally unaccustomed. The communal backbone shivered in delicious horror. Here it was—what the poets and playwrights had been saying all along—plain for everyone to see: woman's unbridled sensuality led to evil consequences. Even the divine Mozart

Illus. 8. The actress Charlotte Wolter posing as Cleopatra for Hans Makart. Photograph.

Illus. 9. Photomontage of Hans Makart shown ten times.

had allowed Sarastro to deliver a similar precept to Pamina—"A man must lead your heart, for without him every woman tends to step beyond her effective sphere" (*The Magic Flute*, Act I, Scene 3). With just one Symbolist picture the rustic moralizer Segantini delivered modern woman up for contemporary judgment. The verdict was in, corroborated internationally by artists from Edvard Munch to Franz Stuck. Woman was sexuality incarnate; let him who trafficked with her beware. For the robust Klimt this proved a pictorial invitation to which he was enthusiastically equal; for Freud, the inveterate explainer, it constituted a basic premise for the universal phenomenon of guilt and repression he discovered in his patients.

The drastic message and unusual nature-versus-humanity format of Segantini's bizarre morality-piece produced an extraordinary impact upon contemporary artists. Reverberations ranged from shameless Viennese imitations, such as Max Kurzweil's (1867–1916) *Death of the Dryad* (Color Plate 11), to sophisticated paraphrases, such as Paul Klee's "sour" etching of 1903, *Virgin in a Tree* (Illus. 10). Whatever the metamorphosis, the overabundance or denial of sexuality remained a common theme. Just as Schopenhauer had engendered philosophical pessimism by his admission of the persistence of evil, so Vienna's male spokesmen for the whole human condition now subscribed to a sexual de-

Illus. 10. Paul Klee, *Virgin in a Tree*, 1903.
Etching. Guggenheim Museum, New York.
Photo: Robert E. Mates.

terminism through their affirmation of a *femme fatale* principle of life. As long as Eros was discussed in terms of eternal male entrapment by unassuageable female sensuality, the sexual merry-go-round would continue its joyless revolutions.

As the Viennese began to drink more and more frequently of the heady wine of eroticism, so recently decanted by Makart and Segantini, the provincial, more stalwart inhabitants of Franz Josef's empire brought with them to the capital a different sort of moral obsession. The painter Albin Egger-Lienz (1868–1926), born in Striebach near Lienz in the Tyrol, is an arresting example. Often called the Austrian Hodler, and close to Segantini in his glorification of humble peasant life, this country artist lived and painted for twelve years in Vienna (1899–1911) without ever succumbing to the *femme fatale* virus. Indeed, his sober *memento mori* themes (*The Dance of Death of the Year 1809*) and aggressive reminders of provincial piety, such as *The Cross* (Color Plate 12), must have seemed like the thunderings of a modern-day Savonarola to the jaded city dwellers. His was a message of impersonal, agrarian determinism, completely at odds with the need of a pleasure-seeking Vienna for hedonistic fantasy.

The piety of Egger-Lienz and the moralizing of Segantini were soon reduced to sermonettes; the thrill of remorse began to fade, leaving eroticism as seductive as ever. And it was to the panorama of sensualism that Vienna's leading artists now turned. Makart's erotica-through-exotica formula had called attention to the excessively painted surfaces of his canvases. In the hands of Vienna's Art Nouveau painters, the surface became a glorious façade, simultaneously concealing and revealing a teasing Eros. This was the sphere in which Viennese fantasy worked most brilliantly: titillation. Koloman Moser's (1868–1918) *Poster for the Fifth Exhibition of the Vienna Secession* (Color Plate 13), with its mellifluous mapping of negative and positive areas, presents a compositional interchangeability that mirrors the androgynous quality of its long-haired,

flat-chested, winged protagonist (a conundrum of gender present also in Peter Behrens' woodcut *The Kiss*, and found in Beardsley as well). Moser's phantasmagorical *Loïe Fuller* (Color Plate 14) was not only a stunningly faithful transcription of the ethereal effects obtained by the American dancer and her "thousand yards" of undulating silk, but also a modern expression of woman as intangible abstract.

Such shimmering chimeric reveries were solidified by the more audacious Klimt. The transitory aspect of corporeal love is indicated above the heads of the embracing couple in *Love* (Color Plate 15) by a cinematographic unfolding of the stages of woman from eager child to emaciated hag. For Klimt the manifest ubiquity of sexuality pervaded even such sacred institutions as law. His allegory *Jurisprudence* (Black and White Plate 10) painted for the Vienna University grapples unforgettably with just this dilemma: the intrusion of the senses into abstract concepts. The stern presences of Law, Justice, and Truth, represented by three small female figures, await an octopus-entangled prisoner at the bar—a wizened, resigned old man escorted aloft by the three Furies, who in their snake-entwined nakedness are far more formidable than the personifications above them. This sort of floating cosmos, with its constellation of human and allegorical figures, its intimations of swamp roots and distant skies (see also Klimt's other two University panels, *Medicine* and *Philosophy*, Illus. 11) appeared to the average onlooker as a "fantastic riddle," while the emphasis on nudity seemed downright licentious (not being invisibly "draped" with history, as were Makart's bacchanals).

Illus. 11. Interior of the XXV Secession exhibition of 1903 with Klimt's panels, *Medicine* and *Philosophy*, Bildarchiv Osterreichische Bibliothek, Vienna.

What the public failed to see in Klimt's fantastic and sober allegory was the quality of interconnection (*Zusammenhang*)[11] between life and death, which, even more than the acknowledgment of universal Eros, was the painter's philosophical message. Although not a deep thinker, Klimt, through his cosmic knots of humanity ascending from chthonian to celestial realms, was programmatically expressing two of the most seductive concepts of his time: Nietzsche's idea of eternal recurrence, affirmed by Klimt as biological regeneration; and the "flux of sensations" theory of experience presented by the physicist Ernst Mach (1838–1916) in his influential Vienna University lectures during the years 1895–98. Klimt's operatic staging of cyclic recurrence adrift in a flow of sensation (see also Color Plate 16, *The Virgin*), and his fatalistic sense of *Zusammenhang* have an almost exact literary parallel in the early writing of Vienna's poet of aestheticism, Hugo von Hofmannsthal (1874–1929). His beautiful "Many truly" ("Manche freilich," ca. 1895) reads like an inventory of Klimt's University panels:

Many truly down below must perish
Where the heavy oars of ships are passing;
Others by the helm up there have dwelling,
Know the flight of birds and starry countries.

Many lie with heavy limbs remaining
Near the roots of life obscurely tangled;
There are chairs meanwhile set up for others
Near to sibyls, queens for their companions,
And they sit there as at home contented,
Easy in their heads, in their hands easy.

Yet from their existence falls a shadow
Reaching the existence of those others,
And the easy are to the burdened
Bound, as to earth and air, together.

I can never cast off from my eyelids
Lassitudes of long-forgotten peoples,
Nor from my astounded soul can banish
Soundless fall of stars through outer distance.

Many destinies with mine are woven;
Living plays them all through one another,
And my part is larger than this slender
Life's ascending flame or narrow lyre.[12]

The public did not need a libretto for Klimt's single-figure icons in the tradition of Makart's prominent *femmes fatales* of the past. Klimt's majestic women came from the Old Testament (two versions of *Judith*, 1901 and 1909) and from classical mythology (*Pallas Athene*, Color Plate 17). The countenances of these new effigies were unmistakably modern (Klimt had followed Makart as Vienna's favorite society portraitist). In the upper

Illus. 12. Herakles Wrestling Triton, mid-6th-century B.C. Attic black figure kylix from Tarquinia, interior. Museo Nazionale, Tarquinia.

right background frieze of *Pallas Athene* a black-figured Attic-vase-derived Herakles wrestles with Triton (Illus. 12).[13] The three females in the picture — the spectator shown in profile on the left side of the frieze, the miniature nude Nike in the goddess's right hand, and the "real life" Athene herself — function as a foil to the painted action. Like Nietzsche, Klimt has thrown off Winckelmann's "noble simplicity and calm grandeur" interpretation of antiquity and has addressed the irrational sexual premise of life.

Klimt's lifelong fascination by the multiple manifestations of Eros should not be interpreted in terms of a battle between the sexes, however. His perception of sexual determinism was not as pessimistic as that of his morose contemporary Munch. Where Munch was threatened, Klimt was exhilarated; where the Norwegian was overwhelmed, the Austrian was speculative. Thus Klimt's great 1903 statement on regeneration, *Hope* (I) (Color Plates 18 and 19), differs substantially from Munch's ambivalent treatment, *Madonna* (Illus. 13). Printed as a color lithograph the previous year, *Madonna* had been bitterly described by Strindberg as a being for whom the accomplishment of the act of conception is "the sole end and justification of this creature, devoid of existence in her own right." Klimt shows not the self-consuming ecstasy proclaimed by both Segantini and Munch but the truism that life and death are equally present in the great continuum of biological renewal. As in his earlier painting *Love*, an "audience" observes the protagonists. The burstingly pregnant, resolute red-haired woman and her sperm-whale-like partner drift in striated currents of water or air in which float ornamental shapes ranging in source from Mycenaean coils to modern cytogenetics.[14] Despite the elemental division of color into ice-blue and

15

Illus. 13. Edvard Munch, *Madonna*,
1895–1902. Lithograph. Museum of Modern
Art, New York.

fire-red, and the wide-eyed expectation of the woman whose hair is spangled with flowers, the specter of death is an endogenous factor in this audacious manifesto.

The Habsburg Dynasty was itself cursed with the specter of death. The brother, son, sister-in-law, wife, and heir of Kaiser Franz Josef (1830–1916) were all to come to terrible ends. Maximilian (1832–1867), his frustrated younger brother who was born "two years too late," became the ill-fated Emperor of Mexico whom Juárez captured and executed by firing squad. Franz Josef's talented but unstable son, Crown Prince Rudolf (1858–1889), thwarted personally and politically by the unbending Kaiser, committed the unpardonable sin of suicide: at the imperial hunting lodge in Mayerling he shot his seventeen-year old mistress and then blew his own brains out. Eight years later the Kaiserin Elisabeth's younger sister, Sophie (1847–1897) — once briefly the fiancée of mad King Ludwig — was burned to death in the famous charity bazaar fire at Paris. The following year Elisabeth (1837–1898) herself was senselessly knifed by an Italian anarchist in front of her Geneva hotel. And on the morning of 28 June 1914, in the Serbian town of Sarajevo, an assassin's bullet pierced the throat of the heir apparent, the Archduke Franz Ferdinand (1863–1914), thus precipitating the massive death spectacle of World War I.

The old Kaiser's aura of fantastic personal tragedy (Illus. 14) and his well-known Spartan habits (he slept on an iron bed every night of his life and breakfasted every morning at five on two unbut-

tered rolls) combined mysteriously to keep alive the dwindling phantasm of the Dual Monarchy. Nor was sensuality absent even from this superbureaucrat's rigid work regime. Rendezvous with Vienna's famous actress Katharina Schratt (1855–1940), to whom the Kaiser dispatched 538 letters and 220 cables during the years 1886 to 1913,[15] were endearing evidence of human imperfection proudly cherished by his people.

Death and sexuality: these two forces continued to propel both the imaginary and the real life of Vienna. What Klimt juxtaposed in fantasy, the Mayerling suicide had verified. The Secession group, of which Klimt had been the first president, continued to exhibit grandiose literary or biblical themes, such as Rudolf Jettmar's (1869–1939) *Lucifer Leaving Cain to His Fate* (Black and White Plate 11) and *Prehistoric Monsters on the Road to Hell* (Black and White Plate 12). But during the first decade of the twentieth century there began to appear a younger group of painters in whose careers death and sexuality would figure with an almost diabolical intensity.

It was this intensity that differentiated the new Viennese Expressionists from their immediate artistic predecessors. Richard Gerstl (1883–1908) (Illus. 15), the son of a wealthy Hungarian Jew, had reason to feel — as did his idol, the musician Mahler — an "intruder" in Franz Josef's Catholic Vienna. Extremely gifted and fiercely impatient with the artistic status quo, Gerstl dismissed the laborious craftsmanship of Klimt's ornate façades. He developed a direct, painterly style based on Velázquez's shimmering white impastos, Van Gogh's agitated surfaces, and the most recent Fauve color explosions. Landscapes and portraits were his subjects, and very quickly the emotional smears of his oil pigment became themes in themselves — almost super-subjects with their own flickering *élan vital*. In his near-obliterations of motif in favor of furor of execution, Gerstl anticipated the abstract expressionism of De Kooning. He also set himself on a collision course with what since 1907 had become his favorite subject matter: the family and person of Arnold Schönberg (1874–1951) (Color Plate 20). Gerstl the uncompromising outsider found an emotional haven in this Jewish composer's avant-garde circle of musicians, and he was accepted as a member of the family — invited to their lakeside summer retreat and even engaged by Schönberg as his painting instructor. There is an undeniable aptness about the originator of twelve-tone musical dissonance laying out colors on his palette under the tutelage of the distortionist of gestalt, Richard Gerstl. Schönberg's own work soon took on hallucinatory aspects (Illus. 16 and Color Plate 21) similar to the expressionistic *Sprechstimme* (talk-sing) effect he achieved in *Pierrot Lunaire* (1912). The Russian painter Kandinsky was quick to recognize the searing quality of his friend's paintings. "Just as in his music, so also in his painting

Illus. 14. Kaiser Franz Josef, 1914. Photograph.

Illus. 15. Richard Gerstl, *Self-Portrait,* detail, c. 1907. Oil. Collection Viktor Fogarassy, Graz.

Illus. 16. Arnold Schönberg, *The Critic,* c. 1910. Oil. Private collection.

Illus. 17. Otto Weininger (1880 – 1903), c. 1903. Photograph.

Schönberg renounces the superfluous (in other words, the prejudicial) and goes directly to the essential (in other words, the necessary)."[16]

Unfortunately, an atonality abruptly sounded in Gerstl's personal relationship with the Schönbergs: all parties concerned were mortified when the painter impetuously declared his infatuation for the motherly Mathilde Schönberg — Arnold's wife. Rejection was immediate and total. Crushed beyond recovery, Gerstl documented the corrosive course of his depression in a haunting series of close-focus self-portrait heads, recalling the autoscopy of Messerschmidt before him (Black and White Plates 4a–d, and 5). But exorcism did not take place for Gerstl, and the pathology of his despair culminated in a double self-destruction: after burning most of the contents of his studio, he put a rope around his neck and, in front of the mirror he had used for his self-portraits, plunged a butcher knife into his heart. He was twenty-five years old. And he was only one of an unusually large number of young intellectuals who chose suicide as the final escape from a Vienna which had become a city no longer of dreams but of nightmares.[17]

It was the young philosopher Otto Weininger (1880–1903) (Illus. 17) and not Freud who through his own bizarre life and writings unleashed the nightmare of Eros coupled with death upon Viennese consciousness. One of Vienna's many Jewish anti-Semites, Weininger hurled his homemade bomb at society in a strange, tormented publication of 1903 entitled *Geschlecht und Charakter* (*Sex and Character*). The 599-page book was a "psychological" world explanation of gender differences in which women (and Jews) were equated with an amoral, passive sensuality, and men with ethical rationalism. This was an unacceptable and tragic antithesis which Weininger believed he saw operating in all persons because of the existence of both feminine and masculine principles within every individual. The reprinting history of Weininger's tract on bisexuality — seventeen editions by the end of World War I — was phenomenal; the impact on the twenty-three-year-old author, forced in this exposition of self to confront his Jewishness and his homosexuality, was fatal. Seeking out the Schwarzspanierstrasse house in which his hero Beethoven had died, Weininger rented a room there and during the night shot himself in the heart. Viennese intellectuals were shaken by this morbid affirmation of the tension and repression toward which opposing traditional values had steered human existence.[18]

But the scientists of the psyche — Freud's brilliant disciple Viktor Tausk (1879–1919) also took his own life in frustration over his relationship with Freud and Lou Salomé — were not the only ones to betray the atmosphere of permanent tension that hung like the enervating Föhn wind itself over Vienna. The most extraordinary fantasy yet to be dreamed in the city of dreams involved not suicide, but mass exodus. This was the fervent fantasy of

Theodor Herzl (1860–1904), the Hungarian-born founder of Zionism. As the Paris correspondent for Vienna's *Neue Freie Presse*, he had witnessed with horror the rising irrational tide of anti-Semitism occasioned by the Dreyfus trial (1894). It was then that he first began to doubt that the assimilation practiced by most urban Jews could really take root in the soil of subliminal racism. Europe was already convulsed by a plethora of subject nationalities clamoring for political independence. Next to the gypsies, the Jews were the most traditionally despised race in Europe. And yet the gypsies had obstinately refused to be absorbed by the Western culture. If the assimilated Jews were to be forever resented because of their cultural and economic prowess, then perhaps a drastic solution should be sought for the "Jewish problem." If the wealthy industrial Jews of Vienna were to be tolerated only on the basis of their financial usefulness to the outspokenly anti-Semitic mayor of Vienna, the popular Karl Lueger (1844–1910) — "I decide who is Jewish" — then why not quit Vienna, the Habsburg Empire, and even Europe altogether? Herzl's escapist fantasy turned into a utopian political proposal: establishment of a Jewish state. Completely possessed by the vision of a separate homeland for his people, Herzl devoted the rest of his life to his cause, imploring the pope and the monarchs of Europe to aid him in persuading the Turkish sultan Abdul-Hamid to grant Jews the right to settle in Palestine. The do-nothing educated liberal Jews of Vienna, including Karl Kraus (1874–1936) who mercilessly lampooned Herzl in the pages of his magazine *Die Fackel*, were either tepid or derisive about Zionism, but the great masses of East European rural Jewry were spellbound by Herzl's magnificent obsession. Civic freedom, deliverance from pogroms, abolition of the need to assimilate, and release from Weininger's and Kraus's brand of self-hatred — these were the seductive components of the fantasy destined, decades later, to become one of the most significant events of the twentieth century. Nine months after the sparsely attended burial of Otto Weininger, whose contempt for his own Jewishness had led to self-annihilation, some eight thousand unbidden persons from all over Europe solemnly followed the funeral cortege of Herzl, Vienna's most visionary dreamer of dreams.

If some forms of Viennese self-hatred could be eradicated through dreams of escapism, such was not the case with another psychological malaise that now seemed to close in upon the emerging Expressionist generation. This was the acute sense of anxiety felt by those who, like Gerstl, had looked through the disintegrating façade of turn-of-the-century aestheticism and beheld an existential nil just beyond. In spite of its last gay efflorescence, a sense of impending disaster imbued the operetta world of the senescent monarchy. The world affliction perceived by a mirthless new generation of artists was translated into a grave intensity. A cult of pathos was born. The psyche under unbearable stress—whether from longing or repression—offered a beckoning terrain for Viennese Expressionism. Intuitively echoing contemporary explorations by the young science of psychology, Expressionist writers and artists plumbed their own and collective anxieties and made the soundings public. Thus an awesome parade of troubled psyches began to form, beginning with Hofmannsthal's vampiric blood-lusting play *Electra* of 1903, Robert Musil's (1880–1942) 1906 novel of adolescent awakening and group sadism at a military boarding school *Young Törless* (*Die Verwirrungen des Zöglings Törless*), and Schönberg's hallucinatory musical monodrama *Expectation* (*Erwartung*) of 1909, articulating the inner thoughts of a woman who frenziedly searches for and discovers the dead body of her unfaithful lover in a forest.

The Expressionist painters added their own poignant images of psyches under stress to this horrific public display, and assured themselves of the widest possible audience through the poster medium. Both Max Oppenheimer, known as "Mopp" (1885–1954), and Oskar Kokoschka (b. 1886) utilized this art form to broadcast urgent messages of pathos. Kokoschka tossed the public a grim summer theater advertisement, *Pietà* (Color Plate 22), in which, posited between the polarities of moon and sun, a Weininger-like battle of the sexes takes place as a crazed woman tears at a flayed man. Mopp's stylized self-portrait in oil *Bleeding Man* (Black and White Plate 13) was used as the basis for a color lithograph poster for his 1911 one-man exhibition, and the epidemic of self-pity became unmistakably individualized when Schiele showed

Illus. 18. Egon Schiele, *Self-Portrait as St. Sebastian*, 1914. Ink, black crayon, and watercolor. Historisches Museum der Stadt Wien.

himself as the martyred St. Sebastian on a placard announcing a 1915 showing of his works (Illus. 18).

But the new pathos concerning death and sexuality could have its ecstatic dream state as well as its nightmarish savagery. Only a year before the creation of his bellicose *Pietà* poster, the twenty-two-year-old Kokoschka had written and illustrated a lyrical work celebrating the attraction between the sexes. This was the prose poem, *The Dreaming Boys* (*Die Träumenden Knaben*, 1908), originally commissioned as a children's story and handsomely published by the Wiener Werkstätte (the Vienna Arts and Crafts Workshop) with eight color lithographs (Color Plate 23, *Eros*). The written and pictorial imagery are both highly stylized, combining a pseudo-naiveté with a sophisticated antirealist array of expressive devices to convey a dreamlike atmosphere. Accompanied by loosely associated illustrations like *Eros*, Kokoschka's text evokes the image of a voyage (awakened adolescent sexuality in search of self-expression). The passionate desire to communicate and experience release is built up through the use of abruptly shifting images, a constellation of sexually suggestive symbols (fish, knife, flower, lake), dislocated phrases and settings, abruptly changing metaphors, staccato outbursts, repeated motifs, and subjective associations. The poem begins aggressively and continues with a reverie:

red little fish
red little fish, i kill you with the three-bladed knife
i tear you apart with my fingers
that there may be an end to the silent circling. . . .

and i fell down and dreamt
many pockets has destiny
i wait by a peruvian stony tree. . . .

female blood furies
who in groups of four and five out of the green
breathing forests by the sea
where it rains silently
crawl away
. . . make waves across forests and
move through the rootless
red-flowered
countless air branches. . . .

. . . oh how i am glad
that you resemble me
how you resemble me
do not come nearer
but live in my house. . . .

. . . the snow flows together into a lake
and on a red little fish you were sitting. . . .

out of your round breast your
breath goes over the blue lake
how quiet is the working of all being
i grasp into the lake and dive into your hair. . . .

19

and i was tumbling
when i recognized my flesh
and was all-loving
when i spoke with a girl[19]

Recent literary precedents for Kokoschka's precocious poem were to be found in Strindberg's "dream" plays of 1902 to 1907, and, nearer to home, Hofmannsthal's sensuous and melancholic voyage imagery in the poem "Experience" ("Erlebnis," 1892), as well as the sudden cruelties of Musil's *Young Törless*. But the closest precedent was the recently deceased French poet Arthur Rimbaud (1854–1891), whose visionary twenty-five-stanza poem "Le Bateau Ivre" ("The Drunken Ship," translated into German and brought out as a popular publication in 1907[20]) was strikingly similar to Kokoschka's poem in its cryptic and colorful metaphors. The Viennese art critic Joseph August Lux sensed the spiritual kinship between the French and Austrian *enfants terribles* and wrote that "the colorful drunkenness of Kokoschka's puberty legend" reminded him of Rimbaud, "with his drunken, unrestrained verses."[21]

Neither the art critic Lux nor the inattentive public took much notice of the rich gestural repertoire performed by Kokoschka's somnambulistic figures in *The Dreaming Boys*. Such angular, awkward body language used as outer manifestation of fulminating inner forces was a first Expressionist intensification of the eurythmic postures found in the allegories of the great Swiss symbolist painter Ferdinand Hodler (1853–1918), of whom a major retrospective had been given by the Vienna Secession in 1903–4. Both Kokoschka and Schiele were to develop the new "ugly" body language of *The Dreaming Boys* into a portraiture of pathos—or of "pathology," as contemporary critics gleefully dubbed it.

Although the "musk"-emanating masturbating woman in the upper right edge of Kokoschka's *Eros* had also slipped by public attention in 1908,

Kokoschka's later sexual fantasies did not. His *Self-Portrait with Life-Size Doll Made in the Likeness of Alma Mahler* (Color Plate 24) was indisputably the most fantastic image yet conjured up by the Viennese imagination. It was all the more audacious in that the fantasy—the doll—was a monstrous reality, an actual object, hand-sewn by a seamstress in Stuttgart after Kokoschka's meticulous drawings and written instructions. His specifications included the doll's mouth ("Can the mouth be opened? And has it got teeth and a tongue?") and the genitals: "… the *parties honteuses* must be made perfect and luxuriant and covered with hair."[22] To comprehend why the "mad Kokoschka" cherished such a fetish, it is necessary to recall that the model was none other than Vienna's own real-life *femme fatale*. Alma Schindler (1879–1964) became Alma Mahler in 1902, Alma Gropius in 1915, and Alma Werfel in 1929. Her marriages were to three of Europe's most famous men—Gustav Mahler, the composer, Walter Gropius, the architect, and Franz Werfel, the writer. She also drew into her orbit, by the sheer magnetism of her "Wagnerian" passions, a constellation of noted intellectuals and artists—filling her "flower garden of geniuses," she called it. Foremost among these rare blooms, during the period from Mahler's death in 1911 to the outbreak of World War I, was Oskar Kokoschka. Years later, in August of 1949 when Alma, widowed for the last time, became a septuagenarian, Oskar wrote her a birthday reminder of what their love had been: "There has been nothing like it since the Middle Ages, for no couple has ever breathed into each other so passionately."[23] In 1958 Alma in turn reminisced: "Years have passed, but the sensations of that time will be equally strong in me as long as I live. On one stormy, agonized day when he loved me passionately, but selfishly, torturing us both, the world around me suddenly melted away...."[24]

Both have left versions of their first encounter and of the fantastic love affair that held Vienna's scandalized attention for three years. It is instructive to read them side by side:

Alma Mahler

"There's a poor, starving genius around," my stepfather told me one day in the winter of 1912. "If I were you, I'd let him paint me." And Oskar Kokoschka came.... But his shoes were torn, his suit was frayed. A handsome figure, but disturbingly coarse, I thought.... His eyes were somewhat aslant, which gave them a wary expression; but the eyes as such were beautiful. The mouth was large, with the lower lip and chin protruding. ... He started drawing again, interrupted by coughing spells. When he tried to hide his handkerchief, I saw blood spots on it. We hardly spoke—and yet he seemed unable to draw. We got up. Suddenly, tempestuously, he swept me into his arms. To me it was a strange, almost shocking kind of embrace; I did

Oskar Kokoschka

My face was thin and drawn and the eyes were too big in it, eyes full of the insolence of an alert will, in contrast with the sleepy people around me. I was beginning to realize what I amounted to. . . . I knew this society lady, a young widow. She wore a purple dress of goffered Venetian silk that was so fine that one could have pulled the whole dress through a wedding-ring. Her hair gleamed like that of the penitent Magdalenes painted by Venetian masters. . . . We went for drives in a carriage with rubber-tired wheels, we sat in her box at the opera, she gave me the key of her house so that I could come and go without being noticed. On summer nights I preferred to climb up the rose-spalier to the balcony leading to her bedroom. . . . There was the awe of the not respond at all.....He stormed out. In a matter of hours I held the most beautiful love letter and proposal in my hands: "...If you can respect me—if you want me to be as pure as you were yesterday...then make a real sacrifice and become my wife; in secret, while I am poor."...The three years that followed were one fierce battle of love....He was jealous of all things in my life.[25]

first human sacrifices, from reluctant yielding all the way to complete abandonment, tumult, quarreling, bliss of self-mutilation until one found oneself again....I would have thought it impossible that at my beck and call the beloved would come, atremble with shameless pleasure....I shut my beloved off from all society, because I sensed a rival in every man.[26]

The possessive Kokoschka did indeed have many rivals to be jealous of, but the strangest competitor of all was the death mask of Gustav Mahler which, at Alma's insistence, traveled with them. The accounts of this fantastic companion run thus:

Alma Mahler

We thought and talked often and earnestly about our future, and Mahler's death mask, which had come by then, made a powerful *canto fermo* for the grave choral chant of these discussions. Wherever I lived after Mahler's death I would put on his desk his music and his pictures from childhood through the last years. One day Kokoschka suddenly got up, picked up Mahler's pictures one by one, and kissed Mahler's face. It was an act of "white magic"—he wanted to combat the dark, jealous urges within him. But I cannot say it helped.[27]

Oskar Kokoschka

When one opens a door there's something on the far side that was not there before. I had a premonition that it would be irrevocable when, from a crate filled with wood-shavings, or curly paper, she unpacked the death mask of her late husband....When the crate with the undesirable contents, the mask, destroyed my love that March day, I clenched my fists and screamed into the dead man's face, that's to say, at this yellowish wax mask with the closed eyes: No, I won't have it, you can't be there between us.[28]

And then the occasions for jealousy were over. World War I began, and with it the end of "the greatest love affair since the Middle Ages":

Alma Mahler

He was obsessed with the idea of marrying me. When he took away my birth and baptismal certificate and I found out by chance that the banns for our wedding had been posted in the Döbling borough hall and the wedding day had been set, I decided to leave town until the day was past....In August we went to Tre Croci in the Dolomites....We lived for his work alone....It was a happy, positive, forward-looking time that was cut short by the news of the assassination of the crown prince and his wife, followed by the Austrian threats against Serbia and finally by the all-destroying fact of war—a war imposed on the entire world. Oskar Kokoschka soon went into the army. Everything was at an end. Oskar Kokoschka had fulfilled my life and destroyed it at the same time.[29]

Oskar Kokoschka

My union with that lady came to the knowledge of those who are so timorously concerned with reputation. Gossip about town made her uncertain of herself. She could not bring the child into the world without first entering into a legal union with me. How could she do that with a young man who had not earned himself a position and a name in society? Without an income, without property! My happiness was already lying anaesthetized upon the operating table and I was still full of superfluous fears that in that helpless state she would seem desirable to a doctor—that's how foolish I was!...In the following days the newsboys in the streets were shouting their special editions. The world war began....After a certain amount of time had passed I volunteered....[30]

At the front Kokoschka received a severe head wound, which ultimately disqualified him from further military service, and in 1917 he fled the city of bittersweet love and settled in Dresden. But the life he led was one of unrelieved loneliness. In spite of an appointment as professor at the Dresden Academy of Art, his war experiences had left him incapable of enjoying human company. Still obsessed with the then unobtainable Alma Gropius, he hit upon his "fetish" idea—the creation of her double. If Alma had her mask of Mahler, he would have his facsimile of her. Alma's memoirs again pick up the story: "Soon I started hearing rumors of [Kokoschka's] crowning eccentricity. He had a life-sized doll made: a figure with long blond hair, and painted—so I was told—completely in my image. The doll always lay on his sofa, and his visitors thought that they were seeing me there in the flesh....At last, he had me where he wanted me: helpless in his hands, a docile, mechanical tool."[31]

And certainly this is what Kokoschka conveys in his bizarre double portrait: his limp, staring partner is nothing but a mindless manikin. What a pyrrhic victory it was to point to her "perfect and luxuriant *parties honteuses*" in empty possession in this picture, the weirdest of all of the fantastic art of Vienna.

No less intense was the fetish of self-pathos and narcissism that gripped Kokoschka's younger colleague, Egon Schiele (1890–1918). He too created a strange and constant companion for himself—a pathetic apparition drawn from the world of illusion and discovered in his own mirror. Self-portraiture was an obsession which dominated the artist's early allegories and portraits. It abated in urgency only slightly during the few years of marriage and artistic recognition before his death from influenza at the age of twenty-eight, just three days after the death of his pregnant wife from the same illness. Death and sexuality played prominent roles in Schiele's tragically short life and were featured aggressively in his prodigious output. As a boy he had witnessed the syphilitic deterioration of his father, who died completely insane when Schiele was fourteen. The "world melancholy" (*Weltwehmut*) with which the young artist invested his autumnal landscapes, anthropomorphic trees, and "dead town" views thus sprang from a childhood clouded by an "unspeakable" tragedy. His own sexual curiosity was enormous and, before his full-length mirror, he explored himself and others rapaciously, leaving trenchant pictorial accounts of his findings. The grotesque Doppelgänger reflected by Schiele's mirror in works such as the *Self-Portrait Nude* of 1910 (Color Plate 25) is much more than a narcissistic double. The emotion-racked torso with its "amputated" arms and lower extremities is a

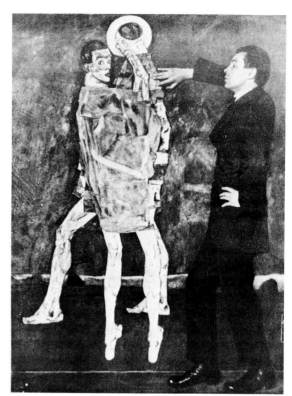

Illus. 21. Egon Schiele in front of his painting *Self-Portrait with Saint*, 1913. Lost.

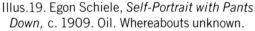

Illus. 19. Egon Schiele, *Self-Portrait with Pants Down*, c. 1909. Oil. Whereabouts unknown.

Illus. 20. Maximilian Lenz, *Marionettes*, c. 1910. Oil. Whereabouts unknown.

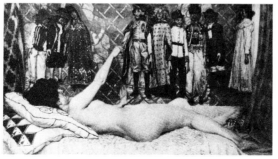

shocking (and exhibitionist) pictorial punishment for "sin." The sin was masturbation. Perhaps because venereal disease caused his father's death, this then-taboo activity both attracted and terrified the artist.[32] Schiele's mirror literally caught him in the act (Illus. 19), his secret exposed and his hands flung in shame to his face. Such confessional sexual spying was disturbingly different from the "acceptable" voyeurism of imperial Secession favorites, such as Maximilian Lenz (1860–1948) in his titillating *Marionettes* (Illus. 20). Schiele's thematic narcissism dealt with masturbation, guilt, and self-inflicted symbolic punishment with the same unsparing relentlessness as that applied by Freud in his pursuit of the unconscious. The hypocrisy and repression of Viennese society provoked both the artist and the physician into penetrating beyond the façade to the psyche. Twentieth-century angst, with its twin Furies of eros and death, was being laid bare.

Like Makart, Schiele was intrigued by the possibilities of photography, and he even posed for a number of extravagantly postured photographs of himself. Combining his real-life image with his painted likeness (Illus. 21), he engaged in a terse somatic dialogue that suggests a remarkable parallel to the broken silhouettes and angular motions soon to be employed by the avant-garde of modern dance, Mary Wigman (1886–1973) and the Bohemia-born Harald Kreutzberg (b. 1902). As Schiele and his contemporaries greeted the new epoch with their psychodramas, the three-quarter tempo of Vienna's waltz world yielded to an inflammatory two-quarter beat while the grim parade of psyches under stress marched onto history's proscenium.

Schiele was the first artist in the thousand-year history of the Habsburg Empire to be imprisoned because of his art. Certainly if the imperial censor had looked closely at Klimt's symbol-saturated canvases, he might have discovered the sexuality beneath the alluring decorative overlays (compare the "accessible" posture of Klimt's *Virgin*, Color Plate 16, with the lofty inaccessibility of Schwind's mountain personification, *Virgin*, Color Plate 3). And it is true that the "color massacres" (Arthur Roessler) of Kokoschka caused the Archduke Franz Ferdinand to recoil with indignation, exclaiming that the artist should have every bone in his body broken. But it was Schiele, with his careless yet willful *épater les bourgeois* ways and his reputation for "pornographic" drawings, who was arrested and sent to prison for twenty-four days. This thoroughly shocking experience, with its revelation that the artist as such was not sacrosanct, triggered an identity hiatus that, still in front of his mirror, the artist sought to fill through a variety of anti-social, self-pitying guises. Petulantly playing the outcast, he portrayed himself in the roles of hermit, monk, or martyred saint (Illus. 18). The anxiety-ridden world view of Expressionism merged with his own, and he found release in biographical "allegories" such as the gruesome *Death and the Maiden* (Color Plate 26), a farewell message in which the artist — as Death — releases himself from a claustrophobic love relationship that had itself gone dead (he was about to marry another woman). After the outbreak of the war, and partly because of the new identity of soldier forced upon him (he was drafted three days after his wedding), Schiele's allegories, although still flirting with the macabre, as in *Mother and Two Children* (Color Plate 27), evinced a genuine and universal pathos that differed noticeably from the exploited, bristling narcissism of his earlier works. His joyless probings of love and death, rendered with mordant linearity and bittersweet colors against a background nil, expressed a particularly Viennese ethos of *Weltwehmut* — born from centuries of combating the real with the unreal, of imaginatively side-stepping the great existential abyss. With the end of World War I, Habsburg Vienna had waltzed over the brink, and of the three Expressionist artists who had dared to look into the chasm, Gerstl, Kokoschka, and Schiele, only Kokoschka was left.

Two other artists, whose beginnings had taken root in the prewar past but whose long careers extended into the second half of the twentieth century, played an important role in the further charting of the fantastic. One was the talented Albert Paris von Gütersloh (1887 – 1973) (Black and White Plate 14). Actor, painter, editor, novelist, scenic designer, and playwright, he became after World War II a respected professor at the Vienna Academy where, with his emphasis on psychic primitivism, he inspired the Vienna School of Fantastic Realism. His contributions to Expressionism include one of the movement's earliest novels, *The Dancing Fool* (*Die Tanzende törin*, 1911), and critical defense of both Schiele's (1911) and Schönberg's (1912) paintings. Gütersloh's dreamy *Self-Portrait at the Easel* of 1913, with its playful repetition of reflected images, is characteristic of the kaleidoscopic density of both his prose and his painting style, anticipating international Surrealism and the Vienna School of Fantastic Realism. The year 1913 was the last year in which one could dream: as the sensuous new tango from South America swept hotly through Vienna, the suicide of Colonel Alfred Redl, a homosexual General Staff officer blackmailed into betraying military secrets to Russia for a period of twelve years, hit the evening papers, and a shocked nation learned that the social pretense it had condoned and codified could conceal a schizoid existence.

It was the rift between appearance and reality that perturbed Alfred Kubin (1877 – 1959) (Black and White Plate 15), the second artist to map out the geography of fantasy from pre-World War I to post-World War II in Austria. Kubin's long life was marked by a compulsion to comment upon himself through writing and by an immense artistic production of a singularly private nature. Thematically his works move from the macabre and grotesque to the eerie and other-worldly (Black and White Plates 16, 17, and 18; Color Plates 28 and 29); stylistically they employ a predominantly black-and-white approach, with an energetic calligraphy based upon the intimate medium of the quill pen and developing from a stressed contour conception to a more tonal articulation. His energies were directed toward articulating the specters that haunted him, and in his autobiographical essays he meticulously described those events of his childhood and adolescence that he believed influenced the character of his art, thus obligingly delivering data for later psychoanalytic interpretations of his work.

Kubin's father's position as a land surveyor took the family to Zell am See, Austria, and it was in the environment of this small Alpine resort that the artist's boyhood was spent. Family preoccupations and his mother's epilepsy prevented much attention being spared for Alfred, and the boy began to compensate by withdrawing into a private world of fantasy. Kubin records that his greatest joys as a child were reading fairy stories and capturing small animals for which he built elaborate cages and miniature torture-racks. He drew incessantly, and the themes of both drawings and daydreams always concerned great catastrophes — storms, fires, and the horrors of war. The death of his mother, when he was ten, did not shock the boy so much as did the grief-stricken conduct of his father, who lifted his wife's corpse in his arms and ran wildly about the house with it. A predilection for the morbid was freely indulged as Kubin, unsupervised, frequented the cattle markets and pig slaughterings and witnessed the occasional dredging up of corpses — suicides and drunkards — from the lake. As a teen-ager he added to his childhood habits (he still kept worms and snakes in cages) all night orgies and heavy drinking. He visited a hypnotist (who had formerly been a butcher, thus especially attractive to Kubin) and submitted to a series of exhaustive experiments. At nineteen he attempted suicide. His preparations were elaborate. Acquiring an old pistol, he studied an anatomy chart to determine just where to direct his bullet, and made a corresponding gash in his head. The locale chosen for his suicide was his mother's grave — so doubly to grieve his father, whom he resented and feared profoundly. But the gun had rusted, and when he pulled the trigger it did not fire. This aborted suicide left his father unmoved, and Kubin volunteered for the army. He served exactly eighteen days before suffering a complete nervous breakdown with convulsions and delirium. During a slow convalescence he began to draw again, and a family friend suggested the therapy of formal art training in nearby Munich, where Kubin arrived with high hopes at the age of twenty-one.

In Munich it was not the academy that determined Kubin's direction but discovery of the erotic work of Max Klinger (1857–1920). Klinger's ten-etching cycle of 1881, *Finding of the Glove*, centered on a woman's glove found by a young man at a skating rink, and the subsequent roles the glove takes in his amorous fantasies, suggesting simultaneous real and dream levels of action. For Kubin, to whom everyday experience took on nightmarish qualities, Klinger's super-veristic scenographies were a stunning revelation. That a private obsession — the multiple erotic connotations of a glove — could be expressed as an *art* theme excited him immeasurably. Here was the sanction (unobtainable from the academic world) for Kubin to utilize his hallucinatory inner world for art. Kubin relates that after seeing the Klinger etchings he roamed through the city in a dazed, half-conscious state and in the evening entered a cabaret where, as the orchestra began to play, he saw the room and customers transformed into a menacing world of babbling beasts. The floodgates of his imagination had been opened.

In real life a bizarre event occurred at the end of 1903 which further aggravated his morose broodings. He had become engaged, and a few weeks before the scheduled wedding, his fiancée died suddenly. Kubin went to pieces, spent his money wildly, and three months later married a young widow whom he had just met. With an unerring Kubinesque sense for tragedy, the artist had chosen a drug addict for his life companion. Her forty-four years with Kubin were plagued by stays in various clinics and a slow death from cancer.

Two further events affected the artist's life and work. In 1906 he acquired the small, isolated country estate Zwickledt, just below Passau, in Austria, which was his home for the next fifty-three years. Solitarily situated in a forest, Kubin's remote little house naturally became the haunted environment in which he sought to encounter and capture his own ghosts. In 1908, after a trip to Italy to distract himself from the recent shock of his father's death, Kubin was seized by a desire to write a "fantastic novel," an obsessive task at which he worked day and night for twelve weeks, followed by another four weeks during which he drew surrealistic illustrations for his manuscript. The result was an extraordinary adventure story, *The Other Side* (*Die andere Seite*, 1909), which, like Gütersloh's *The Dancing Fool*, constituted one of the earliest pieces of Expressionist literature.[33] *The Other Side* is a pre-Kafkaesque (Kubin and Kafka later met in Prague in 1912) depiction of the rise and fall of a secret dream kingdom, The dream kingdom is not a utopia; it is a Boschian land of horrors in which everything is decaying and reality continually shifts appearances — coins turn into ants, temples suddenly collapse, fish fly in the air; only the unhealthy temperament can survive here. The power of Kubin's novel lies in an eerie indistinction between the real and the unreal. With an aberrant unpleasantness that recalls the artist's early drawings, the novel's mood grows increasingly inimical as the uncanny becomes the familiar and everyday events reveal horrifying, demonic dimensions.

Kubin's literary and pictorial imagery unites the two tendencies in Austrian fantastic art: exploration of the mysterious world of elemental forces contained in nature, and revelation of the inner self. Kubin savored the general probing of the other-worldly behind the appearances of reality. He recast it through a process that began as exorcism and ended as interpretive discipline.

With morbid acquiescence Kubin looked forward to his own death. The ten autobiographical sketches he drew around a 1921 photograph of himself when he was forty-four (Black and White Plate 15) are a fascinating assessment of the high points of his life and career. He began with the year 1877, showing himself as a baby; then, proceeding by decades, as the neglected schoolboy of 1887 — the year of his mother's death — and as an eager youth with fishing pole and Alpine hat in 1897 — the year of his army enlistment and mental breakdown. The decade pattern was then interrupted and Kubin showed himself in 1902, the year of his first art exhibition. The next vignette is labeled 1908, the year in which he wrote *The Other Side*. In these latter two self-portraits he is confident and alert. The next year chosen is 1927 — with a question mark below it. Would he still be alive? The four remaining sketches are labeled 1932?, 1937?, -? — with a detailed sketch of the artist on his deathbed, his head lit by two candles — and, finally, 1977, marked by a grin-

24

ning skull. Kubin, the eremite, was nevertheless an imbiber of the Austrian elixir of eros and death, and the vastness of his phantasmagorical oeuvre provided a well-stocked hothouse for generations to come.

Among the more recent artists who have chosen to follow Kubin's black-and-white highway into the fantastic is Hans Fronius (born 1903). Born in Sarajevo, the very town where the shot was fired that put an end to the Habsburg dream, Fronius has steadfastly pursued a universal vision in his art. Like Kubin, he received an academic training — six years at the Vienna Academy — and as with Kubin, it was an outside stimulus that introduced the somber key-signatures in which future work would be set. The discovery at about the age of twenty-two of the paradoxical realm of Franz Kafka (1883 – 1924) challenged Fronius to enter a similar territory in the field of art: "old Austria's" no man's land between the real and the unreal. Fronius's response to Kafka's world ranged from illustrations of his works and imaginary portraits (Illus. 22) to masterful intonations of Kafkaesque moods in the austere charcoal conjurings of swamplands and enigmatic, magical fish. Among those who responded enthusiastically to Fronius's work was Kubin himself. A lifelong friendship ensued, and it was the younger artist, Fronius, who sketched the actual deathbed portrait of Kubin (Illus. 23) on 23 August 1959, after a longevity Kubin had not guessed at in

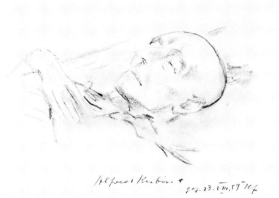

Illus. 23. Hans Fronius, *Deathbed Portrait of Alfred Kubin,* 1959. Black chalk. Albertina Museum, Vienna.

his self-portrait fantasia (Black and White Plate 15). Fronius is a concerned and humanistic observer of the modern aftermath of Kafka's vision of the inscrutable holocaust, and his *Struck by Blindness* of 1977 (Black and White Plate 19) is a compassionate, contemporary parable of the human dilemma.

Compilation of private parables of old and modern times seems to be a common factor in the symbol-saturated, enigmatic, precisionist work of the so-called Vienna School of Fantastic Realism.[34] The founding members of this post-World War II "insurrection" were: Anton Lehmden (born 1929), Rudolf Hausner (born 1914), Wolfgang Hutter (born 1928), Erich Brauer (born 1929), and Ernst Fuchs (born 1930). Their pictorial repertoire of mysterious personages, hybrid metamorphoses, devastated landscapes, quixotic architectural surrounds, and ambiguous "events" is, in a sense, a visual Viennese equivalent to the international Theater of the Absurd. (In fact, Hutter has designed the costumes and scenery for productions of Genet's *The Thief's Journal* and Ionesco's *Bald Soprano*.) Just as the Theater of the Absurd is unthinkable without the precedent of Kafka's fiction, so the Vienna School of Fantastic Realism is inconceivable without the example and actual encouragement of Paris von Gütersloh. Four of the five founding members studied with Gütersloh at the Vienna Academy: Lehmden, Hutter, Brauer, and Fuchs. Exploration of the unconscious — begun by the scientist of the psyche, Freud — has been continued by the Vienna School, and in light of its propensity for an almost rabbinical analysis of the recondite, it is interesting to note that three of the five original members are Jewish: Hausner, whose works were instantly declared "degenerate" by the Nazis after the takeover of Austria; Fuchs, whose parents were victims of the Hitler regime; and Brauer, who as a child was a slave worker for the Nazis. It was from out of the shadows of labor camps and the gaping husks of a bombarded Vienna of 1945 that the modern Viennese *topoi* of the grotesque and absurd arose, or rather, were resurrected, for a fantastic perception of reality had existed ever since the Danube

Illus. 22. Hans Fronius, *Imaginary Portrait of Franz Kafka,* c. 1971. Pen and brush drawing. Collection Hans Fronius, Vienna.

School's intoxicating discovery of elemental nature. Masters of the irrational in nature and in humanity, from Wolf Huber and Altdorfer to Klimt and Kubin, are viewed by the history-conscious members of the Vienna School of Fantastic Realism as their spiritual ancestors. Continuing Klimt's and the Wiener Werkstätte's hand-crafted opulent perfectionism, the Fantastic Realists work with surrealist clarity and intricacy of detail, whether in the fine-lined medium of etching or in the bright prisms and glowing fireballs of oil pigment. A gaily glittering melancholy — typically Viennese in its abyss-filling density — illuminates with extraordinary precision an apocalyptic memory or vision.

Trauma might be the medical explanation for the common heredity and environment of this surprising group of like-minded depictors of the eschatological whose average age at the end of the war had been sixteen. The psychic angst of 1914 had become an open wound by 1945. Each artist responded differently, healing at his own pace.

Lehmden was never able completely to exorcise his war experiences. He is close to Kubin in his preference for black and white, his effusive graphic energy, and his demonic depictions of human strife within a pulsating, ominous nature. Battle scenes sear his memory and his imagery is full of war-scarred landscapes (Color Plate 30).

Hausner typifies the other pole of Viennese fantastic art and is compelled to chronicle not nature but himself. Whether confronting his mirror image as creature of mythology or religion, as Odysseus or Adam (Color Plates 31 and 32), Hausner addresses the endless enigma of identity but meticulously codes his answers into painted conundrums.

Hutter is a modern Ovid, the sensuous surveyor of a magic greenhouse in which the metamorphoses of plants and women can be stopped, speeded up, repeated, or serialized with hallucinatory fecundity. In his *Love-Couple* (Color Plate 33), Hutter presents a union of the sexes in a stagelike setting against a backdrop of swelling botanical forms, each isolated in its own cubicle.

Former folk singer Brauer is a reborn Bosch, whose soft-edged UFO sightings whirl about a vibrant cosmos of glimmering color clusters and flying insects. His fairy-tale moods can convey the sinister as well as the poetic (Color Plate 34), and often they announce a poignant moral (Color Plate 35). Brauer's lepidopteran wars are memories of real battles, however, and recently (1973) the artist devoted himself to painting a cycle concerning the persecution of the Jewish people. Trauma has persisted for this gentle painter of parables who was in Israel during the Yom Kippur War.

Like a thundering Old Testament prophet, Fuchs demands expiation for sins of the flesh. He depicts with Gothic hyperbole the penances in store for humanity, as well as its past temptations and trials (Color Plate 36).

Fuchs and Lehmden are similar to Kubin in their pain-filled, writhing, claustrophobic worlds;

Hausner, Hutter, and Brauer have more in common with the rebus puzzles of Gütersloh, De Chirico, and international Surrealism. Foreboding, a sense of dread, and space surcharged with compound crystalline *things* pervade the works of the Vienna School of Fantastic Realism. The luxuriance of eclectic imagery (drawn, some critics complain, almost exclusively from the Albertina and Vienna Art History Museums), the spewing forth of symbolic and literal data, the blatancy of private sexual confessions, obfuscation of ciphers, and interchange of shapes, titles, and meanings, all speak of a Kafkaesque incommensurability; a veritable Theater of the Fantastic in an unbearably real world in which death and eros still swing each other round as partners in the cyclic dance of existence.

But if the progression of twentieth-century Viennese art of the fantastic has been from the exotic to the erotic, and from the façade to the psyche to calculated pandemonium, there have also been those individuals who have attempted to reverse this awesome process. Arnulf Rainer (born 1929) (Color Plate 37) is perhaps the most important artist to have rejected the Pandora's box opened by the Vienna School of Fantastic Realism. An exact contemporary of the group, his repudiation of their crowded cosmos has also meant an eschewal of his own early work, which originally resembled the figural eruptions of Fantastic Realism. Rainer's Stygian search for a primeval form of painting ("I paint in order to leave painting behind") has its roots in American Abstract Expressionism, and his obliteration of content by gestural overpainting could well be called a Fantastic Abstractionism. For imagery with Rainer is not really destroyed so much as it is overwhelmed, overwhelmed by a great ocean of monochromatic density through which the sunken city can still be glimpsed in its jewellike luster on the shifting ocean floor. Such divination of apparitional counterreality was initially attempted by Rainer in his early "blind" paintings, done with closed eyes. Sheer physical lack of a stretched canvas precipitated Rainer's first (1952) "overpainting" of another artist's completed canvas in a studio where he was, afterwards, a not so welcome guest. The exhilaration of this anti-art act — performed one year *before* Rauschenberg's famous Erased De Kooning Drawing of 1953 — has continued to fuel Rainer's inky trajectory, pulling others into his orbit. Sam Francis, Georges Mathieu, Victor Vasarely, and many other artists have good-naturedly donated finished works for overpainting by the insatiable Rainer. A modern reincarnation of Schiele, Rainer has rushed into the arms of the law (for overpainting without permission a prize-winning work by another artist in a Volkswagen-sponsored competition, 1962). Also like Schiele, but in reverse, Rainer has dealt with his own image — not in order to reveal a psyche but rather to conceal it, literally painting his face and hands with streaks of black paint (Illus. 24). This modernization of Kokoschka's externalized net-

Illus. 24. Arnulf Rainer, *Self-Painting*, 1968.
Photograph. Museum des 20 Jahrhunderts,
Vienna.
Illus. 25. Oskar Kokoschka, illustration for
Murderer, Hope of Women, detail, c. 1910.
Pen and ink drawing.

work of nerves drawn on the skin of his characters in *Murderer, Hope of Women* (Illus. 25) continues the Viennese penchant for *Spiesserschreck* — shocking the bourgeoisie out of their complacency. By creating a new, obnoxious "façade," Rainer has revitalized the urgency of Klimt's deceptively beautiful façades, and has once again implied, through concealment, the fulminating existence of phantasmagorical presences within the nil.

By far the most extreme example of the *Spiesserschreck*, and of the anti-aesthetic strain in the fantastic art of Vienna, is Hermann Nitsch (born 1938). Carrying the Theater of the Absurd to its most gruesome reduction, Nitsch and his Orgy Mystery Theater troupe perform ritual slaughters that involve animal disembowelments and the smearing of blood and viscera over the nude bodies of human participants (Illus. 26). We have observed that death and sexuality have long been the catalysts of Viennese art. At the beginning of the twentieth century Kokoschka pronounced the word "murderer"; in 1914 and again in 1939 mass murder was committed in and by Austria. What Nitsch desires to accomplish in the late 1970s is to obviate further massacres by substitution of a Theater of Violence.

But such visualization of totem and taboo can not take center stage for long in the City of Dreams, where nostalgia chases nightmare and memories of a bittersweet past prevail. It is not the catharsis of a Nitsch, but rather the beguiling escapism of Friedrich Hundertwasser (born 1928) that has most successfully and appealingly joined all the fibers of the fantastic art of Vienna for our century. Hundertwasser's luminous arraslike paintings faithfully reflect the traditional sensuous opulence of his birthplace (Color Plates 38 and 39).

Why did Hundertwasser, coeval and friend of Rainer and the founding members of the Vienna School of Fantastic Realism, develop so distinctively outside the mainstream of post-1945 Austrian art? How did this child of trauma, born with the Christian Czech surname of Stowasser, who served as a Hitler Youth during the same year that sixty-nine of his Jewish mother's relatives were exterminated, avoid incorporating the grim impressions of his youth into his art? Why did he not become a Fantastic Realist, prey to demonic visitations, or at the very least a dynamiter of the vacuum, as did Rainer? A partial answer is that Hundertwasser was born a half-century after his spiritual time. He was and is a turn-of-the-century throwback. Klimt and Schiele are his acknowledged inspirations, the combative Karl Kraus his temperamental godfather. Hundertwasser's indignant public denunciations of the dehumanization of modern "straight line" architecture have included the *Spiesserschreck* technique of lecturing in the nude. And in his periodic abandonment of cosmopolitan Vienna for remote "utopias" such as Morocco, Uganda, Sudan, and New Zealand, he relives Theodor Herzl's willingness to adapt to primitive promised lands.

Hundertwasser resembles the compulsive Kubin in his incessant pictorial production, any time, any place ("I do not have a 'studio' like other painters where paintings are standing around, because I work mostly during my travels in strange places such as coffeeshops, trains, in the grass under trees..."[35]). This modern wanderer carries his bright patchwork bag of Viennese fantasies around the world, and yet his view is calculatedly naïve. Like Paul Klee, whom he admires, Hundertwasser cultivates an "I-Thou" relationship with all visual

Illus. 26. Herman Nitsch, *Ritual Slaughter:
48th Action*, 1975. Photograph by André
Morain.

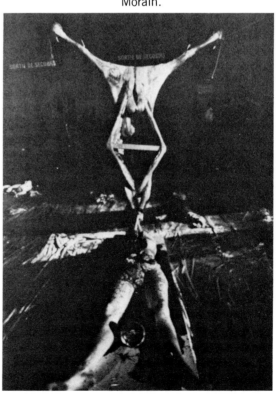

phenomena. His kaleidoscopic chessboard and spiral jumbles of trees, rivers, houses, and faces are a sophisticated recreation of children's art, with its combination of serene wonderment and logical inconsistencies. "Excusez le long regard" ("Pardon My Staring") is the title of a poem the artist wrote in 1953; the same can be said for the people and objects in his multi-faceted pictures: they stare guilelessly at their creator. It is a Hundertwasserian universe of Mach-like filters of stimuli and sensation, woven into a marvelous, bursting, personal plenum. Eros is an often-intoned and desirable presence in the tightly organized rhythmic bedlam of Hundertwasser's multi-patterned microcosms, as in the stunningly beautiful picture *Blind Venus Inside*

Babel (Color Plate 40). The artist's irregular pulsations of silver, gold, green, blue, red, yellow, pink, and white — frequently shown as tears, rain, or blood — are broadcast on a private frequency that beams its emotional, synesthetic message into a black-rimmed maze.

This beckoning maze is recognizable to those who have followed Vienna's fantasy art. It is the previously uncharted spangled cosmos in which Klimt had suspended his great cyclic commentaries on life and death. Thus has the Austrian Daedalus, Hundertwasser, invented a modern labyrinth in which the fantastic art of Vienna can still dance its flight from reality. It may never have to wake from "life's dream to death's wakefulness."[36]

Notes on the Text

[1] The implications of this peculiarity of Viennese patois are raised by William M. Johnston in his encyclopedic study *The Austrian Mind* (Berkeley, 1972), p. 127 and note 34. A popular Viennese Heurigen song confidently expresses the following linguistic fantasy: *Ja, wenn Wienerisch amal a Weltsprach wird, san die ganzen Wörterbüacheln ausradiert* ("Yes, if Viennese were once to become a world language, then all the little dictionaries would be erased").

[2] Alma Mahler, *Gustav Mahler, Memories and Letters* (1946; revised and enlarged edition, Seattle, 1971), p. 109.

[3] Poor Anton Pilgram has had to suffer the scrutiny of art history; this artist's second carved portrait to appear in St. Stephen's Cathedral is periodically denied attribution to Pilgram (see Hans Tietze, *Wien* [Leipzig, 1918], p. 60, p. 88); latest thinking has returned it to Pilgram (Otto Stradal, *Vienna, City of Dreams* [New York, 1973], p. 46). The first sculpted self-portrait, located at the base of Pilgram's carved organ support, has never been disputed as the work and portrait of Pilgram (ca. 1512).

[4] As quoted by Ernst Kris, *Psychoanalytic Explorations in Art* (1952; paperback edition, New York, 1971), p. 130. Kris's analysis of Messerschmidt is heavily Freudian and now quite dated. For an interesting treatment by an art historian, see the article by Lorenz Eitner, "The Artist Estranged: Messerschmidt and Romako," in *The Grand Eccentrics* (eds. Thomas B. Hess and John Ashbery, New York, 1966), pp. 69–83.

[5] Heinrich Laube, as quoted by H. E. Jacob, *Johann Strauss: Father and Son* (Richmond, 1939), pp. 71–74.

[6] Ibid., p. 74.

[7] This was how the ballet was known in Vienna, and I translate from the German title, with its emphasis on "dream," since the original French idea of "release" was — interestingly — not picked up in the title of the Viennese production. For an excellent modern biography of Elssler, see Ivor Guest, *Fanny Elssler* (Middletown, Conn., 1970).

[8] Romako's autobiographical sketch is given in full by Fritz Novotny, *Der Maler Anton Romako* (Vienna, 1954), pp. 115–116.

[9] Edwin Emerson, *A History of the Nineteenth Century Year by Year* (New York, 1901), pp. 1442–45.

[10] See diary entry of 29 April 1912 in Alessandra Comini, *Schiele in Prison* (Greenwich, Conn., 1973), p. 49.

[11] A concept of German Romanticism reintroduced by Ricarda Huch (1864–1947) in her article "Symbolistik vor Hundert Jahren," printed in the issue dedicated to Klimt works in the Vienna Secession's avant-garde periodical *Ver Sacrum* (March 1898), I:3, pp. 7–8.

[12] Translated by Vernon Watkins in *Hugo von Hofmannsthal: Poems and Verse Plays*, ed. Michael Hamburger (New York, 1961), p. 35.

[13] I am grateful to my colleague Professor Karl Kilinski, of Southern Methodist University, for pinpointing the identity of the wrestlers as Herakles and Triton and for suggesting the Attic kylix example reproduced (in reverse) as Illus. 12. I had previously misidentified the mythological scene "quoted" by Klimt as Herakles wrestling with Antaeus in my book *Gustav Klimt* (New York, 1975), p. 21.

[14] Klimt was a good friend of both Zuckerkandls: Berta, the art critic who defended his work in print, and Emil, the anatomist whose Vienna University lectures on "art forms in nature" (inspired by portfolios published between 1899 and 1904, *Kunstformen der Natur*, by the noted German biologist Ernst Heinrich Haeckel) were encouraged by Klimt. The Mycenaean motifs in Klimt were first noted by Jaroslav Leshko, "Klimt, Kokoschka, und die Mykenischen Funde," *Mitteilungen der Österreichischen Galerie* (Vienna, 1969), XIII; Vol. 57, pp. 16–40. Russell Cargo of Southern Methodist University, in his master's thesis on the sources of Gustav Klimt (1977), has discussed the probable impact upon Klimt of contemporary medical illustrations.

[15] This private documentary material has recently been acquired by the Austrian National Library in Vienna.

[16] Kandinsky on Schönberg, in *Arnold Schönberg in höchster Verehrung von Schülern und Freunden* (Munich, 1912), pp. 11–12.

[17] For an excellent discussion of Vienna as a center for suicide, see Johnston, *The Austrian Mind*, pp. 174–180.

[18] The best source for information on the disturbed Otto Weininger is still David Abrahamsen, *The Mind and Death of a Genius* (New York, 1946).

[19] Translation mine.

[20] Rimbaud was greatly prized in Vienna. Schiele's copy of the Insel translation of the poet still bears the artist's appreciative underscorings of "color" phrases in "Le Bateau Ivre" ("Das Trunkene Schiff").

[21] Attention was first drawn to Lux's noting of the affinity between Rimbaud and Kokoschka by Edith Hoffman, *Kokoschka, Life and Work* (London, 1947), p. 38.

[22] Ibid., p. 147. At least nine of Kokoschka's lengthy letters of instruction to the Stuttgart seamstress survive.

[23] Alma Mahler Werfel, *And the Bridge Is Love* (New York, 1958), p. 304.

[24] Ibid., p. 73.

[25] Ibid., pp. 72–73.

[26] Oskar Kokoschka, *A Sea Ringed with Visions* (London, 1962), pp. 24–25.

[27] Alma Mahler Werfel, *And the Bridge Is Love*, p. 77.

[28] Kokoschka, *A Sea Ringed with Visions*, pp. 26–27.

[29] Alma Mahler Werfel, *And the Bridge Is Love*, pp. 78–79.

[30] Kokoschka, *A Sea Ringed with Visions*, p. 29, p. 35.

[31] Alma Mahler Werfel, *And the Bridge Is Love*, p. 132.

[32] Only the briefest discussion of the complex personality of Egon Schiele is possible here. I have given a fuller account of this remarkable artist and his work in *Egon Schiele's Portraits* (Berkeley, 1974) and *Egon Schiele* (New York, 1976); see also note 10 above.

[33] Kubin's important Expressionist novel, *Die andere Seite*, has gone through eight editions in German (the latest, 1962) and was recently translated into English by Denver Lindley (New York, 1967).

[34] The term *Wiener Schule des phantastischen Realismus* was coined by the Viennese art critic Johann Muschik in 1956.

[35] Hundertwasser, in a letter to me of 29 July 1963.

[36] "Vom Lebestraum wohl auf in Todeswachen." Claudio's last line in Hofmannsthal's lyrical play *Death and the Fool (Der Tor und der Tod*, 1893).

Index

30

The Plates

1 Albrecht Altdorfer (c. 1480–1538)
The Wild People of the Woods,
c. 1510. Pen and chalk drawing.
Albertina, Vienna.

2 Anton Pilgram (c. 1460– c. 1515)
Self-Portrait of the Sculptor, c. 1514–1515.
Carved stone pulpit.
St. Stephen's Cathedral, Vienna.

3 Franz Anton Maulbertsch (1724–1796)
Self-Portrait, c. 1760. Oil.
Osterreichische Galerie, Vienna.

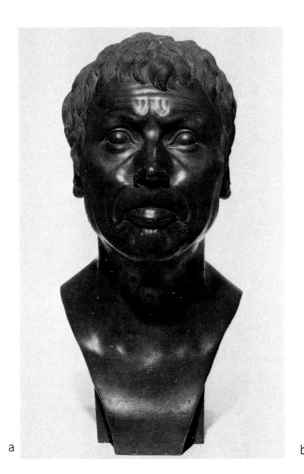 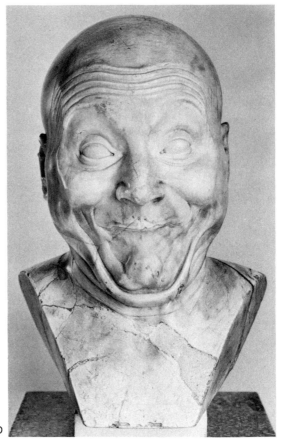

a

b

c

d

4 Franz Xaver Messerschmidt (1736–1783)
Self-Portraits Grimacing, 1776–1783.
Marble and lead.
Osterreichische Galerie, Vienna.

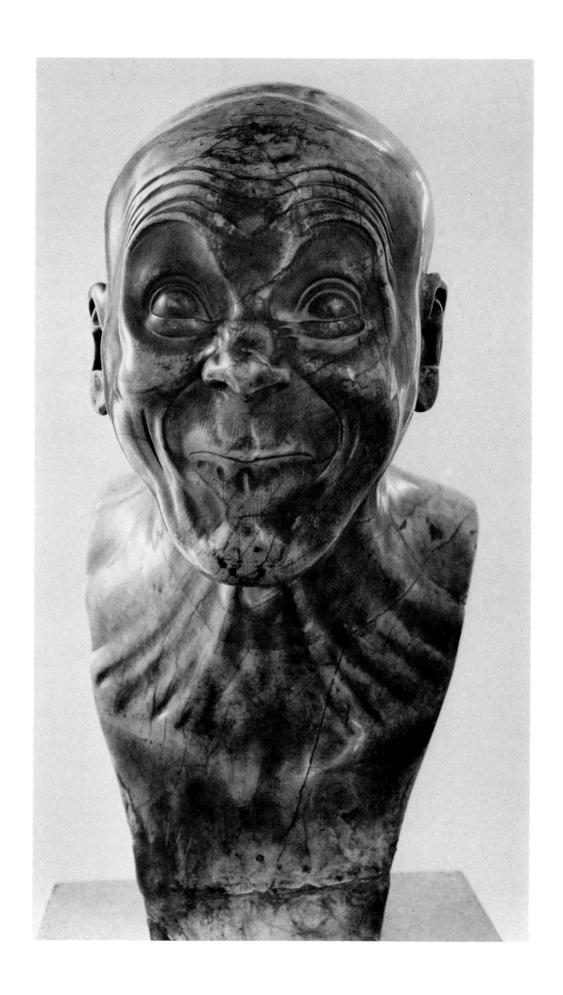

5 Franz Xaver Messerschmidt (1736–1783)
Self-Portrait Grimacing, 1776–1783. Marble.
Osterreichische Galerie, Vienna.

6 Ferdinand Georg Waldmüller (1793–1865)
The Roman Ruins in Schönbrunn Castle Park,
1832. Oil.
Osterreichische Galerie, Vienna.

7 Moritz von Schwind (1804–1871)
The Erl King, c. 1830. Oil.
Osterreichische Galerie, Vienna.

8 Josef Danhauser (1805–1845)
The Art Critics (Dog Comedy), 1841. Oil.
Historisches Museum der Stadt Wien.

9 August von Pettenkofen (1822–1889)
Gypsy Thief Chased by Dogs, 1871. Oil.
Osterreichische Galerie, Vienna.

10 Gustav Klimt (1862–1918)
Jurisprudence, 1903–1907. Oil.
Formerly Osterreichische Galerie,
Vienna, destroyed by fire, 1945.

11 Rudolf Jettmar (1869–1939)
Lucifer Leaving Cain to His Fate,
1919–1920. Etching.
Ostdeutsche Galerie, Regensburg.

12 Rudolf Jettmar (1869–1939)
Prehistoric Monsters on the Road to Hell,
1919–1920. Etching.
Ostdeutsche Galerie, Regensburg.

13 Max Oppenheimer ("Mopp") (1885–1954)
Bleeding Man (Self-Portrait), 1911. Oil.
University of Kansas Art Museum, Lawrence.

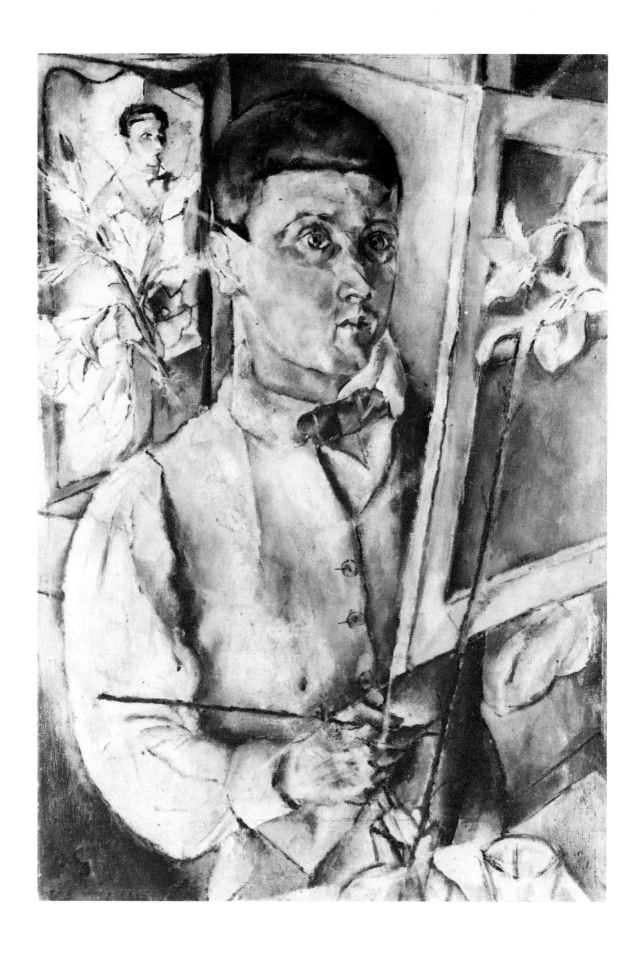

14 Albert Paris von Gütersloh (1887–1973)
Self-Portrait at the Easel, 1913. Oil.
Historisches Museum der Stadt Wien.

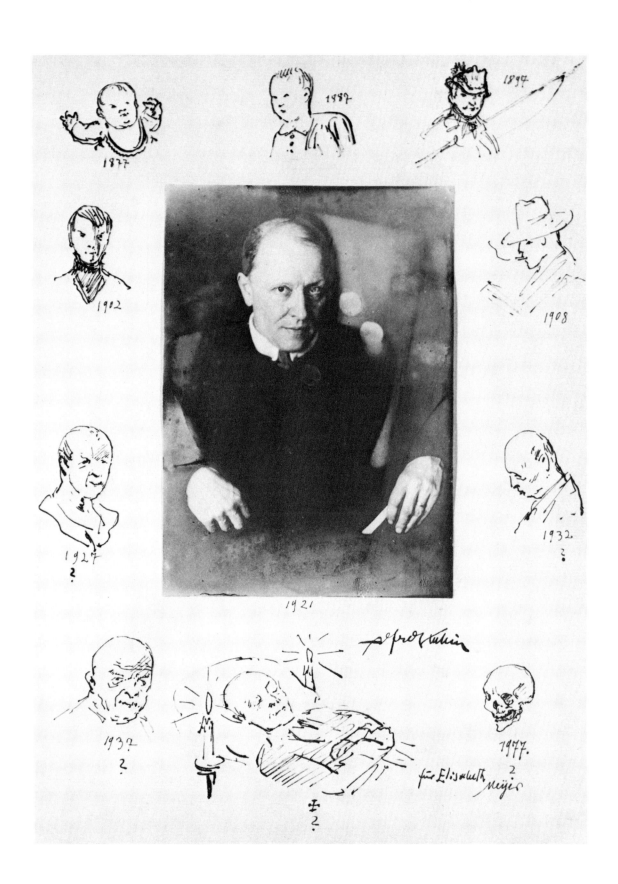

15 Alfred Kubin (1877–1959)
*Self-Portrait Vignettes Around a Photograph of
the Artist*, 1921. Pencil.
Present whereabouts unknown.

16 Alfred Kubin (1877 – 1959)
The Swamp, c. 1900. Pen and wash drawing.
Neue Galerie Linz, Austria. Photo: Spangenberg
Verlag, Munich.

17 Alfred Kubin (1877–1959)
Mother Earth,
1900. Pen, ink, wash,
stipple on "kataster" paper. Private collection.
Courtesy Serge Sabarsky Gallery.

18 Alfred Kubin (1877–1959)
Pipehead, 1945. Aquatint.
Private collection.
Courtesy Serge Sabarsky Gallery.

19 Hans Fronius (b. 1903)
Struck by Blindness, 1977. Etching.
Private collection.

1   Ferdinand Georg Waldmüller (1793–1865)
Boy With Lantern, 1824. Oil.
Kunsthalle, Hamburg.

2   Moritz von Schwind (1804 – 1871)
Rubezahl, 1851. Oil.
Osterreichische Galerie, Vienna.

3 Moritz von Schwind (1804–1871)
The Virgin, 1860. Oil.
Schack-Galerie, Munich.

4   Moritz von Schwind (1804 – 1871)
Erwin von Steinbach's Dream, c. 1859. Oil.
Schack-Galerie, Munich.

5   Anton Romako (1832 – 1889)
The Hot Springs of Gastein in Festival Illumination,
1877. Oil.
Osterreichische Galerie.

6   Anton Romako (1832–1889)
Admiral Tegetthoff in the Sea Battle at Lissa, c. 1880. Oil.
Osterreichische Galerie, Vienna.

7   Hans Makart (1840–1884)
The Death of Cleopatra, 1876. Oil.
Staatliche Kunstsammlungen, Kassel.

8   Rudolf von Alt (1812–1905)
Hans Makart's Studio, 1885. Watercolor.
Historisches Museum der Stadt Wien.

9   Giovanni Segantini (1858-1899)
The Evil Mothers, 1894. Oil.
Kunsthistorisches Museum,
Vienna.

10 Giovanni Segantini (1858–1899)
The Evil Mothers, detail, 1894. Oil.
Kunsthistorisches Museum, Vienna.

11   Max Kurzweil (1867 – 1916)
Death of the Dryad, c. 1898. Oil.
Historisches Museum der Stadt Wien.

12   Albin Egger-Lienz (1868 – 1926)
      The Cross, 1901. Oil.
      Museum Ferdinandeum,
      Innsbruck.

.

13   Kolomon Moser (1868–1918)
Poster for the Fifth Exhibition of the Vienna Secession,
1899. Color lithograph.
Historisches Museum der Stadt Wien.

14   Kolomon Moser (1868–1918)
Loïe Fuller, c. 1900. Watercolor, india ink.
Albertina, Vienna.

15   Gustav Klimt (1862–1918)
Love, 1895. Oil.
Historisches Museum der Stadt Wien.

16 Gustav Klimt (1862–1918)
The Virgin, 1913. Oil.
Narodni Galerie, Prague.

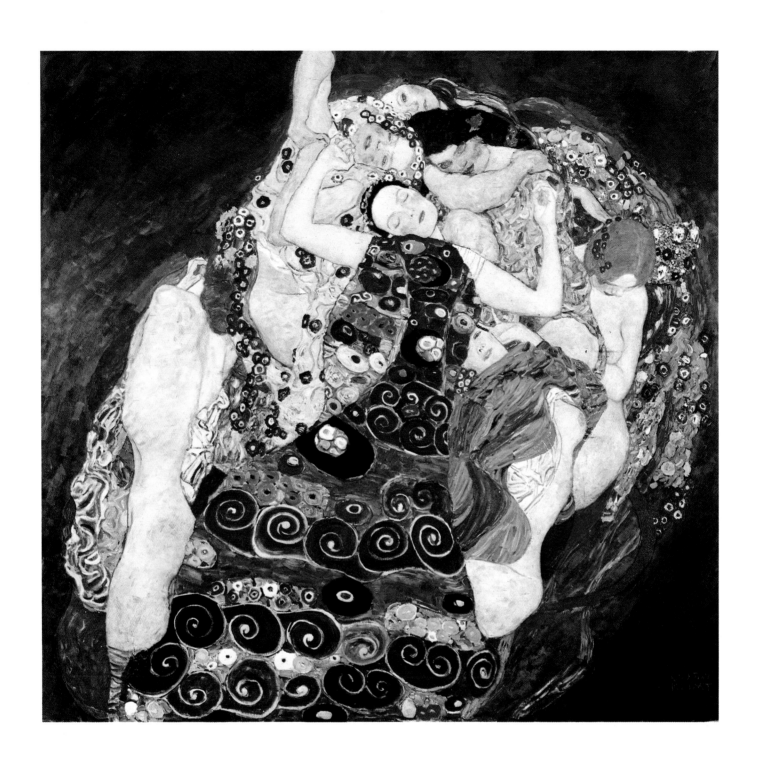

17   Gustav Klimt (1862 – 1918)
Pallas Athene, 1898. Oil.
Historisches Museum der Stadt Wien.

18   Gustav Klimt (1862–1918)
Hope (I), 1903. Oil.
The National Gallery, Ottawa.

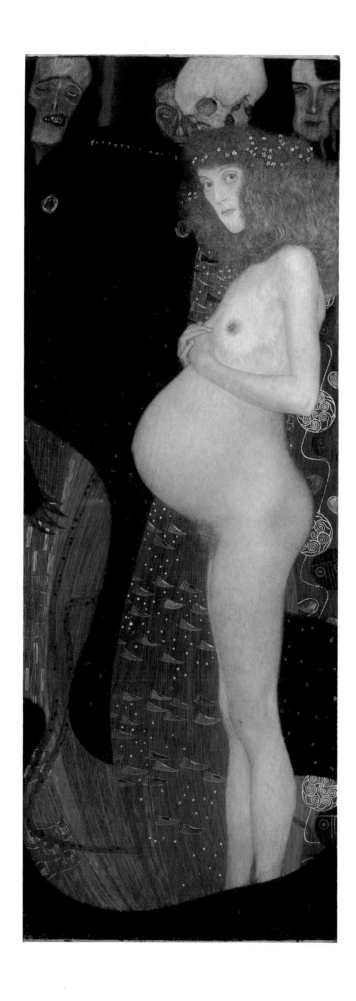

19   Gustav Klimt (1862 – 1918)
     Hope (I), detail, 1903. Oil.
     The National Gallery, Ottawa.

20 Richard Gerstl (1883–1908)
Portrait of Arnold Schönberg and Family,
1908. Oil.
Osterreichische Galerie, Vienna.

21 Arnold Schönberg (1874–1951)
The Red Glance, 1910. Oil.
Stadtische Galerie im Lenbachaus, Munich.
Courtesy of Belmont Music Publishers, Los Angeles.

ARNOLD SCHOENBERG, MAI 1910

22 Oskar Kokoschka (b. 1886)
Pietà, 1909. Lithograph, poster.
Galerie Welz, Salzburg.

23 Oskar Kokoschka (b. 1886)
"Eros," illustration from *The Dreaming Boys,*
1908. Color lithograph. Galerie Welz, Salzburg.

24 Oskar Kokoschka (b. 1886)
Self-Portrait with Life-Size Doll Made in the
Likeness of Alma Mahler,
1922. Oil. Neue Nationalgalerie, Staatliche Museen
Preussicher Kulturbesitz, West Berlin.

25 Egon Schiele (1890–1918)
Self-Portrait Nude, 1910. Black chalk,
watercolor and tempera.
Collection Viktor Fogarassy, Graz.

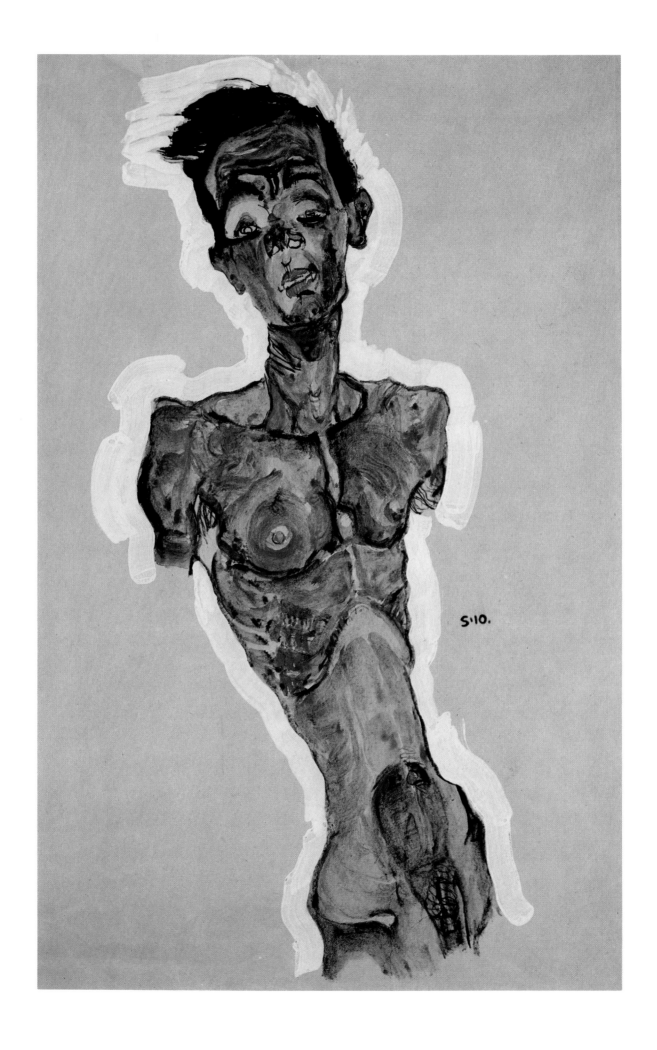

26 Egon Schiele (1890–1918)
Death and the Maiden, 1915. Oil.
Osterreichische Galerie, Vienna.

27 Egon Schiele (1890–1918)
Mother and Two Children, 1917. Oil.
Osterreichische Galerie, Vienna.

28 Alfred Kubin (1877–1959)
The Bell Tower, 1910. Oil.
Pen, ink, and watercolor on "kataster" paper.
Private collection. Courtesy Serge Sabarsky Gallery.

29 Alfred Kubin (1877–1959)
The Laughing Sphinx, 1912–1915. Pen, ink and
watercolor on "kataster" paper.
Private collection. Courtesy Serge Sabarsky Gallery.

30 Anton Lehmden (b. 1929)
War Picture III: Men Fighting in a Landscape,
1954. Oil and tempera.
Museum des 20 Jahrhunderts, Vienna.

31 Rudolf Hausner (b. 1914)
The Ark of Odysseus,
1948–1951.
Tempera and gum colors.
Historisches Museum der Stadt Wien.

32 Rudolf Hausner (b. 1914)
Adam Vis à Vis, 1970.
Tempera and gum colors.
Bundesministerium für Unterricht, Vienna.

33 Wolfgang Hutter (b. 1928)
Love-Couple, 1976. Oil.
Private collection.

34 Erich Brauer (b. 1929)
Tower of Burnt Clay,
1963. Oil.
Collection Joachim Jean Aberbach, New York.

35 Erich Brauer (b. 1929)
*War and Peace Can Be Pulled On and Off
Like Gloves,* 1971–1972. Oil.
Collection Joachim Jean Aberbach, New York.

36 Ernst Fuchs (b. 1930)
*Moses and the Angel of the Lord Before the
Burning Bush,*
1956 – 1957. Oil and tempera.
Bundesministerium für Unterricht, Vienna.

37 Arnulf Rainer (b. 1929)
Self-Portrait ("Rembrandt"),
1969–1970. Oil over photograph.
Private collection.

38 Friedrich Hundertwasser (b. 1928)
The Political Gardener,
1954. Oil on three fitted box-covers made of
fiber-wood, surrounded by a "Baguette electrique."
Private collection.

39 Friedrich Hundertwasser (b. 1928)
Marta Sees Her Friend,
1966. Water-color, egg, oil, aluminum, gold and
copper, polyvinyl on primed paper, glued on hemp
and mounted on canvas.
Private collection.

40 Friedrich Hundertwasser (b. 1928)
Blind Venus Inside Babel,
1975. Mixed technique: egg-tempera, polyvinyl, oil,
tinfoil with Uhu-glue on white priming on chipboard.
Private collection.

is a landmark study of one of the most extraordinary — yet least known — flowerings of modern art.

The art of the Vienna Fantastic Movement, taking on at various times the forms of Art Nouveau, Expressionism, and Surrealism, speaks to us today with arresting force — and in this, the first volume to gather and interpret the masterpieces of that movement, the forty superb color plates present a panorama of images that are at once startling and ravishing. Here, faithfully reproduced, are representative examples of the work of such recognized masters as Klimt, Schiele, Kokoschka, and Hundertwasser, as well as major works by less familiar artists, including Erich Brauer, Ernst Fuchs, Rudolf Hausner, Alfred Kubin, Richard Gerstl, Hans Makart, Anton Romako, Moritz von Schwind, and others. And forty-five additional plates, in black and white, show us further examples of the work of these and other artists, and document the artistic, social, and historical context out of which their work developed.

In her text, the celebrated art historian Alessandra Comini brilliantly interprets the fantastic art of Vienna in terms of the great dualities of Viennese culture: reality and illusion, death and sexuality, the external world and the inner self. With the insight, originality, and wit that characterized her works on Klimt and Schiele, she recreates the milieu in which the artists worked, giving us Vienna itself — the City of Dreams — brooding and tragic, but also richly sensuous and wildly romantic. She gives us, as well, a dazzling view of personalities, events,